THE MAN
BEHIND
THE BOOK

❧ ❧ ❧

Honorable Men
Diary of a Yuppie
Skinny Island
The Golden Calves
Fellow Passengers
The Lady of Situations
False Gods
Three Lives
Tales of Yesteryear
The Collected Stories of Louis Auchincloss
The Education of Oscar Fairfax

NONFICTION
Reflections of a Jacobite
Pioneers and Caretakers
Motiveless Malignity
Edith Wharton
Richelieu
A Writer's Capital
Reading Henry James
Life, Law and Letters
Persons of Consequence:
Queen Victoria and Her Circle
False Dawn: Women in
the Age of the Sun King
The Vanderbilt Era
Love Without Wings
The Style's the Man

THE MAN
BEHIND
THE BOOK

❦ ❦ ❦

LITERARY PROFILES

LOUIS AUCHINCLOSS

HOUGHTON MIFFLIN COMPANY

BOSTON NEW YORK 1996

Copyright © 1996 by Louis Auchincloss
All rights reserved

For information about permission to reproduce selections from
this book, write to Permissions, Houghton Mifflin Company,
215 Park Avenue South, New York, New York 10003.

For information about this and other Houghton Mifflin trade and
reference books and multimedia products, visit The Bookstore
at Houghton Mifflin on the World Wide Web at
http://www.hmco.com/trade/.

Library of Congress Cataloging-in-Publication Data
Auchincloss, Louis.
The man behind the book : literary profiles /
Louis Auchincloss.
p.   cm.
ISBN 0-395-82748-5
1. Authors — Biography. 2. Literature, Modern —
History and criticism.   I. Title.
PN451.A94   1996
809'.04 — DC20   96-19047
CIP

Printed in the United States of America
QUM   10   9   8   7   6   5   4   3   2   1

Book design by Melodie Wertelet

"Dumas *fils*," "Sarah Orne Jewett," "The Abbé Mugnier" and
"Iris Origo" were originally published in *The New Criterion*,
and "Lord Bryce" in *American Heritage*.

For my good friend

THEODORE C. ROGERS,

who has brought a living theatre of classics

to the youth of New York City

❧

Contents

❧ ❧ ❧

ix

Introductory Note

⋇ ⋇ ⋇

The writers discussed have little in common except, as in most compilations of literary essays, that each, at one point or another of my life, has meant a great deal to me as a reader and writer. Many of them no longer enjoy today the vogue they enjoyed in their lifetime, and in these cases it has been my interest to explore the reasons for their fall from grace and seek the portions of their work that may still merit attention. It is impossible for all worthy artists to survive, particularly in a world that produces, with its expanding population, so many more of them than ever before, and it behooves us to carve out of too unwieldy a body of work what should not be lost.

THE MAN
BEHIND
THE BOOK

❧ ❧ ❧

CYRIL TOURNEUR

❧   ❧   ❧

C YRIL TOURNEUR (1580?–1626) can hardly be said to have had a literary life, as we know very little about his life at all. There are scholars who even doubt that he was the author of the two plays traditionally attributed to him, "The Revenger's Tragedy" and the much inferior "Atheist's Tragedy," printed in 1607 and 1611, but I choose not to enter this fray, being firmly convinced, on grounds of style alone, that T. S. Eliot was correct in his conclusion that both plays were the work of one man and that man not any of the other Jacobean dramatists. So to me he is the Cyril Tourneur who was reputed to have been in the service of the powerful Cecil clan and to have gone as a soldier to the Lowlands, and to have died of a plague while on the naval raid of the Spanish fleet in Cádiz. Beside the two tragedies he was also the author of some miscellaneous items of poetry and prose, including an elegy on the death of Prince Henry, heir to James I. Except for "The Revenger's Tragedy," written presumably when he was in his twenties, there is little to deduce that he led a literary life at all.

Marcel Schwob, the French poet, has fantasized that Tourneur was "born of the union of an unknown god with a prostitute" in a day of darkness, in a year of plague of which his mother died, and that "the door of the little house in which he was born was scrawled over with the fatal cross of red, while the mournful tolling of a bell heralded the approach of the ghastly, creaking tumbril which did service for a common hearse."

T. S. Eliot quite properly deplores this as literary criticism, but it does represent a natural speculation as to what sort of man could have written "The Revenger's Tragedy," that flaming, gripping, hideous vision of life, unique even in an age of gory melodrama. Eliot himself admits that "the play is a document on humanity chiefly because it is a document on one human being, Tourneur; its motive is truly the death motive, for it is the loathing and horror of life itself. To have realized that motive so well is a triumph; for the hatred of life is an important phase — even, if you like, a mystical experience — in life itself."

The violence of the play's language tends to find its way into the prose of the critics who admire it. Here is Swinburne:

> There never was such a thunderstorm of a play: it quickens and exhilarates the sense of the reader as the sense of a healthy man or boy is quickened and exhilarated by the rolling music of a tempest and the leaping exultation of its flames. The strange and splendid genius which inspired it seems now not merely to feel that it does well to be angry, but to take such keen enjoyment of that feeling, to drink such deep delight from the inexhaustible wellsprings of its wrath, that rage and scorn and hatred assume something of the rapturous quality more naturally proper to faith and hope and love.

And Allardyce Nicoll, describing the opening scene of "The Revenger's Tragedy" in his beautiful edition of Tourneur, is all but carried away:

The setting is a gloomy hall, oak-panelled and tapestry-hung, in a Renaiscence palace. Two servants, bearing their sputtering torches aloft, lead in a strange procession: a grey-haired Duke, in whom the lines of age are cruel and hard — his Duchess, whose form is florid and voluptuous — his son whom debauchery has already made old — and the Duke's bastard, hatred and envy gleaming from his eyes. The fluttering flames of the torch-light catch their evil faces as they pass by; stray rays of light, too, search fitfully into the dimmer reaches of the hall, and in their search succeed faintly in outlining a dark figure, muffled close and staring madly at the group now moving into the corridor beyond. In his hands, deep-clasped lovingly and bitterly to his bosom, this dark figure clutches something white and ghastly, which a sudden turn of a departing torch reveals as a woman's skull.

The dark figure, of course, is Vindice, the revenger, and the skull is that of the woman he loved and whom the duke had secretly poisoned for rejecting his lewd advances. Now, that is certainly a wrong justifying the most savage revenge. But the point that Eliot makes about the play is that the duke's crime hardly justifies the horror that Vindice and his brother Hippolito feel for the whole world in which they live. Eliot emphasizes that the "cynicism, the loathing and disgust of humanity are immature in that they exceed the object." In this, the play is comparable to "Hamlet," where the hero's disgust at the Danish court (at least before he discovers that his father has been murdered) is hardly justified by the simple fact of his widowed mother's admittedly hasty remarriage.

This excess of disgust is important in any search for the personality and literary intention of the author. Certainly the ducal court in "The Revenger's Tragedy" is a corrupt one. But as the play opens, the wrong inflicted upon Vindice, though terrible, is a single one. Otherwise the court has not touched him. It is alleged that his late father had lacked advancement and died bitterly in genteel poverty, but it is never made clear to what extent the duke or his court were responsible for this. The duke's son and heir, Lussurio, will soon attempt to seduce Vindice's sister, Castiza, a killable offense in Jacobean drama, and will ignorantly employ Vindice, now disguised, to be his pandar, but Lussurio never succeeds: Castiza remains as pure as her name implies.

Nor do any of the other crimes in the unfolding drama affect Vindice's honor. The duke's youngest stepson rapes the wife of an elderly noble, and Vindice's brother and confederate, Hippolito, joins those who pledge revenge, but the raper suffers execution by a double miscarriage of justice without their having to act. The duke's bastard, Spurio, commits adultery with the duchess and plots to kill the heir; the heir plots to kill him, and the duchess's two older sons plot to kill the heir and then each other. Vindice appears to conclude from this concatenation of intended crimes that the murder of his beloved was really the deed of a rotten society rather than of its sovereign alone, and he brandishes her skeleton as a doom to the world he proceeds to obliterate in a welter of killings.

What brought on in Tourneur such a loathing of man? He had served in the Low Countries and must have seen the carnage of war and the frightful atrocities of religious persecution, but these are not the horrors that excite him. It is corruption at court that appals him: the lust for gold and women. Yet he was surely too young and low of rank to have been a courtier of James I, and anyway he was a loyal servitor of the Cecils, who had brought that monarch to the throne. What he seems to have hated most was sexual promiscuity, which was only the indirect cause of his protagonist's wrong, but which was a common anathema, not only in Shakespeare's later plays, but in many of the tragedies of the first decade of James's reign.

The bastard Spurio in "The Revenger's Tragedy" inveighs against his origin with all the gusto and hatred of Edmund in "King Lear":

> Duke, thou didst me wrong, and by thy act
> Adultery is my nature.
> Faith, if the truth were known, I was begot
> After some gluttonous dinner, some stirring dish
> Was my first father, when deep healths went round,
> And ladies' cheeks were painted red with wine,
> Their tongues as short and nimble as their heels,
> Uttering words sweet and thick; and when they rose, —
> Were merrily disposed to fall again, —
> In such a whisp'ring and withdrawing hour,
> When base male bawds kept sentinel at stair-head
> Was I stol'n softly; O damnation met
> The sin of feasts, drunken adultery.

And Vindice waxes almost hysterical in invoking the sins of darkness:

> Night, thou that look'st like funeral heralds' fees,
> Torn down betimes i' the morning, thou hang'st fitly
> To grace those sins that have no grace at all.

Now 'tis full sea abed over the world,
There's juggling of all sides. Some that were maids
E'en at sunset are now perhaps i' the toll book.
This woman in immodest thin apparel
Lets in her friend by water; here's a dame,
Cunning, lays leather hinges to a door,
To avoid proclamation; now cuckolds are
A-coining, apace, apace, apace, apace.

I think Eliot is exactly right in seeing the play as the work of a very young man: "It does express — and this, chiefly, is what gives it its amazing unity — an intense and unique and horrible vision of life; but is such a vision as might come, as the result of few or slender experiences, to a highly sensitive adolescent with a gift for words."

It is like a young man to be so carried away by a hymn of hate as to brush aside until the very last lines of his play any idea that his hero may be going too far in his wreaking of vengeance. Many persons die in the course of Vindice's operations who have done him no wrong at all, and I feel it may have been at the stage director's insistence that some acknowledgment of this had to be made in the end. Just before the final curtain, with the stage piled with bodies and no evidence available to convict Vindice, he suddenly confesses to the murder of the duke and is led away to execution. This was in accordance with church doctrine that "Vengeance is mine, saith the Lord."

But the scene is a flat one, and Vindice does not sound like Vindice. Swinburne was indignant at critics who found in his plea to the new duke — that he had killed the old one "all for your grace's good" — an apparent change of character:

"But if this seems incompatible with the high sense of honor and of wrong which is the mainspring of Vindice's

implacable self-devotion and savage unselfishness, the unscrupulous ferocity of the means through which his revenge is
worked out may surely be supposed to have blunted the edge
of his moral perception, distorted his natural instinct, and
infected his nobler sympathies with some taint of contagious
egotism and pessimistic obduracy of imagination."

In "The Atheist's Tragedy" Tourneur seems to have made
his peace, if a rather shabby one, with that portion of public
opinion which held that tragedies of revenge should condemn
revenge. The hero submits meekly to the savage dictates of
the villain who has wronged him and is saved only when the
latter, taking on the job of executioner, kills himself by accident with the axe he has raised to chop off his victim's head.
Presumably this is by divine intervention, but it makes for a
ridiculous ending. We want our Tourneur undiluted.

Prosper Mérimée

ใช้ ใช้ ใช้

P ROSPER MÉRIMÉE (1803–1870) is one of those writers
whose lives, at least in France, have aroused as much
interest as their works. His enigmatic personality has engendered constant curiosity and considerable antagonism. He
was aloof, remote, with perfect but faintly disdainful manners;
his clipped, terse remarks were interspersed with surprisingly
scabrous anecdotes; he seemed to condescend to his fellow
men. And he was always disappointing people; he had a habit
of switching sides disconcertingly. He started his career as a
political radical; he ended it as the devoted courtier of Napoleon III and the opponent of any extension of the suffrage.
He began as an atheist, but with the onset of old age he wrote
to a friend, "I find myself thinking often of God and a future
existence," and he professed himself unopposed to a religious
service at his death. A lifelong bachelor and frequenter of
brothels, a notorious *coureur de femmes*, he yet loved one mistress devotedly for decades and was heart-broken when she
deserted him. And finally he was a passionately romantic
writer who nonetheless shaped his plots and his prose with a
classical rigor.

He was the son of Léonor Mérimée, a mediocre but cultivated artist who, after nine years of study, received a second

prize in Rome for his painting *Nebuchadnezzor Slaying the Children of Zedekiah,* and thereafter became perpetual secretary of the Academy of the Beaux Arts in Paris. Prosper studied but never practiced law and then turned to literature. He had some success with short stories of tense plots and bloody episodes, written in a tight vivid style, but his first notable achievement was a historical novel inspired by Scott, *Chronique du Règne de Charles IX.* Most of his literary work, including his masterpieces, *Carmen* and *Colomba,* was completed before middle age.

The hero Saint-Clair, in his short story *La Vase Étrusque,* seems to have had a good deal of the young Mérimée in him. Saint-Clair "was not loved in what is called the world, primarily because he only sought to please those who pleased himself . . . He may have been born with a tender and loving heart, but at an early and impressionable age he had allowed his too expansive sensibility to incur the raillery of his comrades." As a result, he "learned to suppress all outward manifestations of what he regarded as weakness of character."

Mérimée was always an enthusiastic dilettante, widely read, a prober into history, a voracious traveller and sightseer, a student of human nature, even in its grisliest aspects. "Don't believe I have a predilection for the mob," he wrote to a friend. "It is simply that I love to study different kinds of manners, a wide variety of faces, and other languages. Though I know the ideas behind them are always the same." His particular hobby, however, was French history, and this led in 1834 to his appointment as inspector general of Historical Monuments, a job that involved exhaustive and exhausting trips all over the country. To his great credit he attempted — though by no means always successfully — to limit the architect Viollet-le-Duc to the restoration of what *had* been and not to the substitution of what *might* have been, but at least he managed to save many crumbling and neglected edifices from total ruin.

The elevation of Louis Napoleon to the imperial throne in 1853 brought about another great change in Mérimée's life. The Comtesse de Montijo, widow of a Spanish grandee and mother of the new emperor's selected bride, Eugénie, was, if not Mérimée's mistress, something much more important to his way of thinking: a friend of the heart. He once wrote: "It's impossible to have a real friend of one's own sex (we men care too much about being 'manly'), and devilishly hard to have one of the other — the devil is always intervening." With Madame de Montijo, however, he definitely succeeded, as the hundreds of letters to her in the dozen or more volumes of his published correspondence clearly show. Renan maintained that Mérimée would have been a man of the first order had his friends not usurped so much of his time and energy, but there are critics who believe that his long and beautiful letters to his intimates constitute his greatest contribution to literature. And those to the new empress's mother are among the best.

Mérimée had known Eugénie de Montijo from her childhood; he loved her almost as a daughter and she him as a kind of indulgent and benevolent godfather. She induced her husband to make him a senator, and he became a faithful attendant at her court for the seventeen years that the empire lasted. Here we glimpse him through the eyes of a new tutor to the young Prince Imperial:

> Entering the fountain court I perceived the empress coming out of the English garden, accompanied by an old gentleman whose eyes were fixed on the paving stones. He was smartly dressed, almost coquettishly so: gray pants, white vest, a sky blue cravat, old style. A large nose with a

square tip — rather odd looking — four deep wrinkles in his brow, a hard cold eye under thick lashes, a flashing pince-nez. Stiff, very stiff. An English diplomat? The empress presented me. It was Mérimée.

He became intimate with the emperor as well and even came to esteem him, though the courtier's wish may have been parent to this judgment. He wrote to a friend: "His ideas are sometimes bizarre but always original. He has a singular talent for gaining one's confidence; he knows how to put people at their ease. He is always polite and benevolent, though always reserved."

Unfortunately for Mérimée, Louis Napoleon's particular hobby, which he pursued with great seriousness, was writing a scholarly biography of Julius Caesar, and he relied heavily on Mérimée's researches. I say unfortunately for Mérimée, as he otherwise might have written his own life of the Roman general and commentator, and a considerably better one. He had to accompany his tireless emperor on a torrid and exhausting expedition to the excavation site of Alesia where Caesar had besieged Vercingetorix and to speculate with him on the minutest details of Roman fashion and clothing. Mérimée used to say that Napoleon's military expertise had better qualified him as the historian of Caesar's campaigns than university professors, but the debacle of Sedan would seem to contradict this.

Mérimée died in 1870, after a long and debilitating illness, and he was not spared the final bitterness of the Prussian victory and the flight of his beloved empress to England.

Colomba is his most remembered piece of fiction, though this distinction might have been earned by *Carmen* had the latter tale not been smothered by Bizet's more popular operatic version. Orson, the hero of *Colomba*, has returned to his native

Corsica, after serving gallantly in the army of Napoleon I and participating in the Battle of Waterloo, to hear his sister's excited version of their father's death: that he has been assassinated by members of a family with whom theirs has been feuding for generations. Orson is not convinced by her wild allegations; absence has emancipated him from the bloody quarrels of his native isle, and he wishes to pursue in peace his courtship of the lovely English heiress he met on the boat coming home. But when he is at last convinced that a crime has indeed occurred, and when he finds himself ambushed by his treacherous foes, he slays the two principals with a couple of perfect shots and wins the hand of the English lady.

His sister, Colomba, splendidly drawn, completely dominates the book. She is the symbol of old Corsica, savage and sly and superstitious, fanatical in family loyalty, an amazon in conflict, the most passionate of friends and the fiercest of enemies, but always beguiling. Inevitably, she makes the English lady, Miss Nevill, seem prim and proper. All of Mérimée's sympathy goes out to her and to her brave brother and even to the two outrageous outlaws who befriend and aid them. He is obviously charmed by men and women who are willing to die for the smallest point of honor, and he loves to contrast the culture in which they flourish to one of money-grubbing businessmen.

But Mérimée in his later years had lost much of his youthful zest for violence and derring-do. He had travelled too widely and observed too much carnage and suffering. He had lived through the street scenes of the revolutions of 1830 and 1848 and served in the militia. He now applauded the order and discipline of the empire. Bloodshed was relegated to the field of romantic fiction, and even there it was strapped in the casing of a beautiful style.

We see him towards the end of his life, in 1865, as he

appeared, at an evening at the Princesse Mathilde's, to the sharp but unsympathetic vision of the Goncourt brothers:

> He listens to his own voice as he talks, which he does slowly, with mortal silences, word by word, drop by drop, as if he were distilling his effects, causing a sort of icy chill to fall all round him. No wit, no epigrams; just a recherché turn of phrase, the diction of an old actor taking his time, with the hint of the impertinence of a spoiled conversationalist, an affected disdain for all illusion, modesty, social convention. For decent-minded people, there is something hurtful in this dry and spiteful irony, deliberately evolved to startle and dominate women and other weak creatures.

ANNE BRONTË

⁂ ⁂ ⁂

A NNE BRONTË (1820–1849) owes such readers of her two
novels, *Agnes Grey* and *The Tenant of Wildfell Hall*, as she
still has, largely to the fame of her older sisters, Charlotte and
Emily, and to the sad and romantic legend of the family of
Haworth Parsonage and the Yorkshire moors. She is generally seen as the youngest, mildest and sweetest of the sisters,
bravely resigned to the humiliations of being a governess in
haughty families and to the agony of consumption and early
death. Her humble hymns to the Almighty and her loving
care of her alcoholic brother, Branwell, in his deliriums have
raised her to near sainthood. But I do not believe she has
been accorded her proper rank as a novelist.

The piety that makes the major flaw in her fiction probably came from the extra dose of Methodism that she got
from her maternal aunt Miss Branwell, who took her dead
mother's place in the Reverend Patrick Brontë's household
and whose particular favorite, as the baby of the family, she
was. All her life she seems to have been hounded by a fear of
hell, and, since she was a generous soul, this fear was manifested more for others than for herself. The brightest heaven
would have been darkened for her by the thought of a single
soul suffering below. Happily, there is evidence in her writ-

ings that she got over this superstition at the end. But it was a formidable load to carry through life.

What particularly emerges from a close study of her fiction, and especially from the autobiographical pages of *Agnes Grey*, is the impression of her strength of character. Far from being meek, she was quite the equal of Charlotte, and she was even stronger than Emily, in that she could cope readily with the outside world. She spent more time as a governess than either of them, as she did not accompany them to the Pensionnat Héger in Brussels, and she learned to endure the snobbish treatment of her employers and the rudeness of their servants without compromising her dignity or her independence. She also learned to observe and record the doings of high life with an eye that missed nothing and a pen that spared no one. Her charges probably saw her very much as the young Murrays saw their governess, Agnes Grey:

> She was very obliging, quiet and peaceable in the main, but there were some things that put her out of temper; they did not much care for that, to be sure, but still, it was better to keep her in tune, as when she was in a good humour she would talk to them, and be very agreeable and amusing sometimes, in her way, which was quite different from mamma's, but still very well for a change. She had her own opinions on every subject, and kept steadily to them — very tiresome opinions they often were, as she was always thinking of what was right and what was wrong, and had a strange reverence for matters connected with Religion, and an unaccountable liking to good people.

And see how scathing Anne could be about a minister whose heart was dedicated more to Mammon than to God.

... and the still less edifying harangues of the rector, who would come sailing up the aisle, or rather sweeping along like a whirlwind, with his rich silk gown flying behind him, and rustling against the pew doors, mount the pulpit like a conqueror ascending his triumphal car; then, sinking on the velvet cushion in an attitude of studied grace, remain in silent prostration for a certain time; then, mutter over a Collect and gabble through the Lord's Prayer, rise, draw off one lavender glove to give the congregation the benefit of his sparkling rings, lightly pass his fingers through his well-curled hair, flourish a cambric handkerchief, recite a very short passage, or perhaps a mere phrase of scripture, as a headpiece to his discourse, and, finally, deliver a composition which, as a composition, might be considered good, though far too studied and too artificial to be pleasing to me.

Agnes Grey may not be quite what George Moore extravagantly called it, "the most perfect prose narrative in English literature," but it has great charm. It is, however, on *The Tenant of Wildfell Hall* that I believe Anne's chief claim to be an important novelist must rest. Charlotte thought that Anne had misguidedly undertaken to write the book as a grim duty to warn the world to teach its young men to avoid the terrible death by drugs and alcohol of their brother Branwell, and there is certainly truth in this, but Charlotte failed to appreciate in her sister the equally important motive of a born writer to write for the sheer love of writing and to give pleasure to others. There is a great deal of that evident in the novel.

All three Brontës were devoted to the first person singular as the best means of telling a story; of their seven novels only

Charlotte's *Shirley* is not related by a narrator, and it is the least animated and forceful of them all. Charlotte did not trouble herself to explain why her heroines were exposing their private lives to the reader ("Reader, I married him," exclaims Jane Eyre); and this is just as well; any excuses, such as diaries or letters, are artificial, and readers will always forgive the "I" as an age-old device. Henry James, it is true, learned to distrust it, but his was always a very special case.

Both Emily and Anne did, however, resort to explanations. The story of *Wuthering Heights* is related by Mr. Lockwood, the rich young Londoner who has leased the Grange in Yorkshire from Heathcliff, who occupies the craggy old manor house on top of the neighboring hill. Lockwood calls on his rough landlord and is rudely treated, and on his way home on a winter night he catches a serious cold, which keeps him in bed for days while his housekeeper, Nelly Dean, entertains him by recounting the history of the families that lived in both houses. This, of course, is the novel, except for the brief finale, related by Lockwood, who tells of his return to Yorkshire after six months in London to find Heathcliff dead and the old feud between the families reconciled. Emily's device is wholly successful. Nelly Dean fits perfectly into her story, in which indeed she plays an important role; she adds the notes of common sense and humor and kindness needed to mollify and place in perspective the rigors and terrors of the events she has witnessed.

Anne in *The Tenant* uses two narrators. Gilbert Markham, the hero, in middle age as the novel opens, is writing to his brother-in-law to tell him the whole story of his youthful romance with the beautiful widow who became his wife. This is a bit of an initial bump to the reader; it seems unlikely that this very "outdoorsy" and prosperous farmer should settle down to indite some hundreds of pages to a relative about his most intimate experiences. But once the story is launched, one forgets the device; one is carried along by the swift prose of the narrative.

Gilbert Markham, like all the Brontë heroes, is very much a man, robust, handsome, humorous, the cock of the walk in a small but admiring neighborhood, carrying on a careless flirtation with a pretty but mean-spirited local girl, busy with his farm, his horses, dog and guns, dominating a sassy kid brother, adored by his widowed mother and sister. All is changed by the sudden arrival in the long unoccupied, tumbledown Elizabethan mansion, Wildfell Hall, of a beautiful, mysterious widow, Mrs. Graham, and her small son. Markham almost immediately falls deeply in love with her, but it is with a new sort of passion, hitherto unknown to him. He regards her as a kind of goddess, and the fact that he knows nothing about her background and that she firmly holds him off and tells him nothing only increases his awe and ardor.

Then the neighborhood rumors begin to fly around: she has no husband, even a dead one; she is the mistress of the owner of the hall; her child is a bastard. Markham fiercely denies every allegation; he is alienated from all his old friends by his angry partisanship; nothing matters to him but his blind faith in Helen Graham. And when he stumbles upon some damning evidence that seems to point to the truth of the gossip, he assaults and almost kills the poor man who is supposed to have been Helen's lover and resolves to see her no more.

The contrast of the mysterious Wildfell Hall and the homey comfort of the Markham farmhouse is reminiscent of that between Wuthering Heights and the Grange. The change in

Markham as he senses the new depth in his life and awareness of things and his wild despair when he feels defrauded of this greater happiness effectively introduce the crisis of the novel, when Helen produces for her angry admirer the diary that will clear her. She lets him read it because she is now in love with him.

The diary constitutes the bulk of the balance of the novel. The difference between it and Markham's letter to his brother-in-law is that it is kept from day to day; the writer can never know what the morrow will bring. It tells the story of Helen's marriage to Arthur Huntington (Graham was an alias), the charming rich idler with whom she was infatuated and whom she married over the advice of an aunt who suspected his wild ways. It is a long, probing, detailed and almost clinical account of the degeneration of a man's character and body through the abuse of alcohol and drugs, but it is made absorbing by the drama of his wife's suffering from the abuse and riotous conduct of her spouse and his boorish houseguests. At length she comes to hate him — Anne pulls no punches about this — but she continues to work for his physical and moral salvation. In the end, however, she flees to an anonymous safety to save her son from being contaminated by a father who seeks to make the child drink.

The reader knows, of course, that she *will* get away, for he has read Markham, but he doesn't know what may happen if Huntington should discover her hiding place. The story is rendered tense when Huntington finds the very diary we are reading and learns of her plan of escape. The diary ends where Helen has torn it out of its book, for she is too shy and modest to let Markham read of her warming feelings for him. The last entry that he reads takes us back to our and the diarist's first impression of him:

November 3rd. — I have made some further acquaintances with my neighbors. The fine gentleman and beau of
the parish and its vicinity (in his own estimation at least) is
a young . . .

The reading of the diary is followed by a meeting between
Helen and Markham and a mutual declaration of love. But it
is also a final meeting; they must part; she has a living husband. Word comes soon, however, that he is dying, and
Helen departs to nurse him in his final illness. Markham
hears of her only through her letters to her brother, and
news of the death of the wretched Huntington, repentant at
the end, is clouded by the unwelcome news that his beloved
is now a very rich woman. Dare he propose to an heiress?
This may seem an unnecessary scruple, but the novel makes
it understandable. There *is* a big gap in their social statuses,
and Helen is too shy to bridge it on her own and too prone
to attribute Markham's failure to do so to indifference. In the
end, had not her son spied Markham from the carriage as he
was walking down the drive of her great house, determined
to leave her forever, there might not have been a happy
ending.

Why then has this beautiful novel been so underappreci-
ated? Because of the unpleasantness of its subject matter?
But that kind of thing is surely the staple of modern fiction.
No, I am sure the hurdle in the way of the book's popularity
lies in the heavy overloading of the Huntington chapters
with religious sentiment. Helen never relaxes in her duty to
save her husband's soul from hell, and the pages are damp
with her sermons to him and her reflections on the parlous
state of his and his friends' souls. There is no question that
Anne intended that her novel should bring a strong moral

message to the reader. As she wrote in the preface to the second edition:

> I would not be understood to suppose that the proceedings of the unhappy scapegrace, with his few profligate companions I have here introduced, are a specimen of the common practices of society — the case is an extreme one, as I trusted no one would fail to perceive; but I know that such characters do exist, and if I have warned one rash youth from following in their steps, or prevented one thoughtless girl from falling into the very natural error of my heroine, the book has not been written in vain . . . Such humble talents as God has given me I will endeavour to put to their greatest use; if I am able to amuse, I will try to benefit too; and when I feel it my duty to speak an unpalatable truth, with the help of God I *will* speak it, though it be to the prejudice of my name and to the detriment of my reader's immediate pleasure as well as my own.

But do not let us forget, as Charlotte was apt to, that Anne was always mindful of her ability to *amuse*, and amuse us she does in the greater portions of her novel, though *not* in passages where her heroine exhorts her erring husband, as follows:

> "God is Infinite Wisdom and Power, and Goodness — and Love; but if this idea is too vast for your human faculties — if your mind loses itself in overwhelming infinitude, fix it on Him who condescended to take our Nature upon Him, who was raised to Heaven even in His glorified human body in whom the fulness of the godhead shines."

We read that in answer to this Huntington "only shook his head and sighed," and the reader can only do likewise. I have little doubt that, with the ample use of a red pencil and without adding a single word, I could turn this novel into the best seller it was in 1848 and still should be.

DUMAS *fils*

☙ ☙ ☙

T HERE ARE OCCASIONAL events and personages in
French history that make one wonder whether the nation can ever be fully understood by a foreigner. One such is
the Dreyfus affair. That a man should be falsely condemned
for espionage is not in itself so strange — what country has
not witnessed the miscarriage of justice? But that the people
of the supposedly most cultivated of nations should be so di-
vided by the effort to rehabilitate the accused that a goodly
portion of its conservative element should wish the conviction
to stand *even if* it were proven wrong seems something that
could not happen, at least in the United Kingdom or the
United States. We had our Sacco and Vanzetti, but did even
those furthest to the right wish to see innocent men electro-
cuted? If any did, they were careful not to say so. Yet in
France there were many who did not hestitate to voice the
opinion that the reputation of the army had to be maintained, even at the cost of injustice to one of its officers. A soldier can be asked to die for his country: should he not be
willing to be disgraced for it?

No! is our resounding answer. Perhaps because we haven't
that much faith in the army. Perhaps because we haven't that

much faith in anything. But does the Dreyfus case make us want that kind of faith?

On the literary side, the huge theatrical celebrity of Alexandre Dumas *fils* (1824–1895) in his lifetime is another case in point. As André Maurois put it in his biography of the father and son:

> It is difficult for us today to realize the precise nature of the position occupied by Dumas *fils* in the Paris of the 'eighties. Not only was he all powerful in the theatre; he also dominated the Academy. The president of France would send for him to his box to congratulate him after a performance. A Dumas *fils* first night had become an event of national importance.

And what is left today of the plays that entranced the French capital during four decades? Only *La Dame aux Camélias*, and that mostly in its operatic and cinematic versions, *La Traviata* and *Camille*. And what is left of the author's lofty preachments and stern moralizing about adultery and prostitution? Only Henry James's beautiful description of the love affair in *La Dame*:

> It is all champagne and tears — fresh perversity, fresh credulity, fresh passion, fresh pain. We have seen it both well done and ill done, and perhaps more particularly the latter — in strange places, in barbarous tongues, with Marguerite Gautier fat and Armand Duval old. I remember ages ago in Boston a version in which this young lady and this young gentleman were represented as "engaged": that indeed for all I know may still be the form in which the piece most finds favor with the Anglo-Saxon public. Noth-

ing makes any difference — it carries with it an April air: some tender young man and some coughing young woman have only to speak the lines to give it a great place among the love stories of the world.

James added immediately to this effusion: "If I have stopped to be myself so much reminded, it is because after and outside of *La Dame aux Camélias* Dumas never really figured among us all again." By "us" he meant himself and his American cousins, but he might as well have included the whole of the Anglo-Saxon world. "We like to be good; the French like to be better. We like to be moral; they like to moralize."

There was a marked and indeed much publicized difference between Dumas's life and his preaching. His tumultuous love life included many adulteries, and, a bitter bastard himself, he fathered at least one natural child. Such flagrant inconsistency may be attributed in goodly part to the major role that his magnificent but prodigal father played in his life. Dumas *père* was simply impossible. He gave his son every reason to resent and despise him — and then charmed him out of his resentment. He allowed his son to bear the social stigma of bastardy, though nothing but caste prejudice prevented him from marrying his mistress; and then tore the child, at the tender age of seven, from the arms of his loving mother by force of law and sent him to a pension, where he was scorned for his irregular birth. Yet the child could never sustain his anger against a parent so exuberant, so charming, so willing to admit faults, so famous, so popular, so wildly generous — in a word, so overwhelming. As Maurois put it: "The father was bursting with health; the son frequently suffered from physical and mental crises which at times even threatened his reason. The father, in spite of his many disappointments, remained an optimist to the end; the son, in spite of much precocious success, died a pessimist."

The son was not even allowed the grudge of being eclipsed as a writer by his best-selling father. Dumas *père* was immensely proud of the brilliant boy, and nobody applauded more vociferously at the crashing success of *La Dame*, when the son was still in his twenties, than the world-renowned author of *Monte Cristo*. Dumas *fils* was welcomed, so to speak, to the family dais.

However much the son may have disapproved of the paternal follies and extravagances, he found himself drawn into a similar pattern of life. "My boy," the older man reminded him solemnly, "when one has the honor to bear the name of Dumas, one lives on a grand scale: one dines at the Café de Paris, and one never says no to a pleasure."

The son had his famous affair with Marie Duplessis when he was only twenty-one. He described his camellia lady as "one of the last of those rare courtesans who had a heart," but the cost of a single evening with her was enough to ruin the young Alexandre. Though already suffering from the consumption that was to kill her, she was kept by millionaires and spent a hundred thousand gold francs in a year. Yet it was he, and not she, as in the popular novel he wrote about her (before turning it into an even more popular play), who broke it off. "My dear Marie, I am neither rich enough to love you as I would wish, nor poor enough to be loved by you as you would." He could not afford her alone, and he refused any longer to share her with others.

Two facts — one, that this affair had introduced him to the greatest ecstasy of his life, and two, that his written interpretation of it had brought him fame and fortune — must have given food for bitter rumination to a mind so lashed by conscience. As he grew more familiar with the Paris world of fashion, he became increasingly disgusted with it, until it began to take on for him the dimensions of a modern Babylon, which it was his manifest duty to admonish and correct. His dramas in the next three decades, however ingeniously plotted and suspenseful, however scintillating with wit and epigrams, and however popular, were nonetheless sermons that his audiences adored without feeling any need to apply them to their daily lives. Henry James has well described them:

> He is exuberantly sincere: his good faith sometimes obscures his humor, but nothing obscures his good faith. So he gives us in their order the unworthy brides who must be denounced, the prenuptial children who must be adopted, the natural sons who must be avenged, the wavering ladies who must be saved, the credulous fiancés who must be enlightened, the profligate wives who must be shot, the merely blemished ones who must be forgiven, the too vindictive ones who must be humored, the venal young men who must be exposed, the unfaithful husbands who must be frightened, the frivolous fathers who must be pulled up and the earnest sons who must pull them.

Life in short presented itself to Dumas "as a battle between the woman and the man."

Young men in the Second Empire, he argued, had become hard; the women provocative. The father in *Un Père Prodigue* says of the son's generation: "Your heart has no use for conquests — only acquisitions. If by some chance a woman of any distinction should fall in love with you, she must yield her body as fast as another would sell it. Young men, young men, you have killed love!" But hear the son on the opposite sex:

"Women's shame has evaporated with the *décolleté* gown. You don't realize that the murmur of admiration that greets the sight of your bare shoulders is an insult in disguise."

What is the answer to this war of the sexes? Dumas was clear: a love marriage between a sexually experienced male and a virgin.

> No woman, however beautiful or well-loved, can give to her love the hundredth part of the emotion which in a single moment a husband receives from the young bride he has chosen when love is first revealed to her. His heart and spirit find in that first expansion of a timid, unknowing but still curious soul a sensation so absolute that it destroys everything that is not she, so complete that it can never be duplicated.

Mightn't that "still curious" have indicated to Dumas that there was something wrong with his formula? The idea that it may have been unfair to require that both, and not merely one, of the spouses be virginal would not have occurred to most of his contemporaries, but shouldn't it have occurred to so fierce a moralist? And we shall see that in time it did.

His greater leniency for men was based, of course, on his belief, then almost universally held, that sexual promiscuity was a natural, even a normal condition for a young male, but not for a female. A man might boast, even complacently, that he had to exercise strong will to curb his lusts; a woman would be most indiscreet to do so. One can imagine Dumas's shrug on learning of a state of sustained virginity in a young male adult: *"Quelle espèce de pédéraste!"* Even the righteous and God-fearing father of Armand Duval, in *La Dame aux Camélias*, asserts: *"Il faut que tout jeune homme ait une maîtresse."* Note the *"il faut."* There are no ifs and buts about it. The only crime would be in *marrying* the mistress. So prostitution is built into the social system, like slavery in the old American South, and the moral code must be adapted to accept it. The fatal crack that this causes in the code did not appear to Dumas until near the end of his life.

If the woman accepted her status as a prostitute and did not aspire to become a wife, she might be redeemable, like the lady of the camellias, who, after all, had a heart. But she was rare. Dumas added a note to his novel: "It is not my conclusion that all prostitutes would have behaved as did Marguerite." More typical to his mind, no doubt, was Suzanne d'Ange, the demi-mondaine of *Le Demi-Monde*, who is determined at any cost to achieve social respectability by marrying a besotted young army officer who is ignorant of her tarnished past. In this he is frustrated by the hero, Olivier de Jalin, a friend of her proposed victim, who to outwit her uses every trick in the pack *except* the revelation of their own old affair — which his honor, suddenly fastidious, prohibits. Perhaps due to a suspicion that at least some of his audience might sympathize with an unfortunate woman trying to better herself, Dumas makes Suzanne a good deal wickeder than the situation really requires. Henry James pointed this out:

It is the means that Olivier uses that excite the wonderment of the Anglo-Saxon spectator. He takes the ground that in such a cause all means are fair, and when, at the climax of the play, he tells a thumping lie in order to make Madame d'Ange compromise herself, expose herself, he is pronounced by the author *"le plus honnête homme que je connaisse."* Madame d'Ange, as I have said, is a superior woman; the interest of the play is in her being a superior woman. Olivier has been her lover; he himself is one of the reasons why she may not marry Nanjac; he has given her a push along the downward path. But it is curious how little this is held by the author to disqualify him from fighting the battle in which she is so much the weaker combatant.

When Dumas came to write *La Femme de Claude*, he threw all restraint to the winds and created a woman so vile, not only in her ruthless promiscuity but in her betrayal of her nation to an enemy, that the hero, her husband, is justified in shooting her dead. Dumas answered his critics in a pamphlet even more violent than his play.

Women never listen to reason; not even to proof. When they do surrender it is always to feelings or to force. They must be either in love or cowed; either Juliet or Martine! Nothing else is of the slightest interest to them. I am writing, therefore, for the instruction of the male. If, after this revelation of the truth, men still persist in making mistakes about women, it will no longer be my fault, and I shall do as Pilate did . . .

Was there, then, no way for a woman with a past to start again? Well, yes. In *Les Idées de Madame Aubray* a woman who has borne an illegitimate child but who has ever since led a life of the strictest modesty, virtue and seclusion is permitted at last by a matron of broad social views to wed her noble-minded son.

Towards the end of his life Dumas began to have some mild sense of the impossibility of any strict application of his views. He had published his plays in an edition in which each piece was harnessed to a lengthy preface announcing its moral, which Henry James had likened to going to a dinner party accompanied by a pair of constables. But now he began to see that the trouble lay quite as much with his men as his women. If the lust of man had created prostitution, then man must learn to contain his lust. Why had Christ conquered the world, he asked his friend Léopold Lacour.

"Because He died on the cross for preaching a doctrine of universal charity and love," came the answer.

"No doubt, but chiefly because the preacher of love died a virgin."

And his next play, which he didn't live to write, was to have been called *L'Homme Vierge*.

It would have made him at least consistent. But Shakespeare knew that the idea could be dramatized only in comedy. In "Measure for Measure" the Viennese law against fornication is seen to be unenforceable.

Today we have liberated both sexes, morally as well as legally. People may do anything they desire, so long as they are of age and consent; they needn't marry and they needn't stay married. Our freedom has engendered other problems, of course. Even animals fight in the mating season. But at least we're not hypocrites.

Has there ever been a society that espoused Dumas's ideals? Perhaps the Massachusetts Bay Colony in the 1640s. I submit this complacent passage from the journal of Governor John Winthrop.

At this court of assistants one James Britten, a man ill affected both to our church discipline and civil government, and one Mary Latham, a young woman about 18 years of age, whose father was a godly man and brought her up well, were condemned to die for adultery, upon a law formerly made and published in print. This woman being rejected by a young man whom she had an affection unto, vowed she would marry the next man that came to her, and accordingly, against her friends' minds, she matched with an ancient man who had neither honesty nor ability, and one whom she had no affection unto; whereupon soon after she was married, divers young men solicited her chastity, and drawing her into bad company, and giving her wine and other gifts, easily prevailed with her, and among others this Britten, but God smiting him with a dread palsy and fearful conscience withal, he could not keep secret, but discovered this.

The woman proved very penitent and had deep apprehension of the foulness of her sin. The man was very much cast down for his sins but was loth to die and petitioned for his life, but they would not grant it, though some of the magistrates questioned whether adultery was death by God's law. They were both executed; and died very penitently, especially the woman, who had some comfortable hope of pardon for her sin, and gave good exhortation to all young maids to be obedient to their parents and to take heed of evil company.

John Winthrop does not seem to have been afflicted with any of the doubts of Dumas *fils*. But at least his serenity spared him from going to such extremes as did the French dramatist when he blamed the defeat of France by Prussia in 1870 on the prevalence of prostitution in Paris!

LORD BRYCE

※ ※ ※

W HEN JAMES BRYCE presented his credentials as British ambassador to President Theodore Roosevelt in 1907, he probably knew more about the nation to which he had been accredited than any foreign envoy in Washington before or since. He had made seven trips to the United States, the first in 1870; he had visited every state; he had studied the federal Constitution and that of each state; he had made himself an expert on Congress, on the state legislatures, on the judiciary and on the party system; and he had extensively interviewed hundreds of American citizens. His classic work, *The American Commonwealth*, first published in 1888, had been reissued again and again on both sides of the Atlantic, and it was taught in schools and colleges here until it was finally out of date. Bryce's friend Theodore Roosevelt felt about him as did his sovereign, Queen Victoria, whom he once accompanied on an Italian vacation as minister in attendance. "I like Mr. Bryce," she observed. "He knows so much and is so modest."

Bryce is still read today by students of history and occasionally by law students for his illuminating analyses of constitutional law as it was interpreted a century ago, but inevitably his work has ceased in the large to be relevant to modern problems, and his is the usual fate of commentators on the passing scene, even when they are as brilliant as Walter Lippmann and as informative as John Gunther. But he has an abiding place in the history of Anglo-American relations. He assisted importantly in the development of the great friendship between the two nations that at last succeeded the long bitterness of the Revolution, the War of 1812 and the misunderstandings and animosities aroused by our Civil War.

Bryce had one of those long, sunny, healthy rich Victorian lives, spread over law, literature, travel, mountain climbing, Parliament and diplomacy, beginning in 1838 with his birth in Belfast of Scotch-Irish middle-class parents and ending, eighty-three years later, in 1922, with a peaceful death on his beautiful estate near London, laden with honors, honorary degrees, the Order of Merit and a viscountcy.

His family had moved to Glasgow in 1846, when his father received a call to teach in a high school there. Bryce attended Glasgow College and then Oxford, where he attained every available honor. He then read law and engaged in a small practice in London, but his primary interests were in literature and politics. In 1864, at just twenty-six, he leapt into fame with the publication of *The Holy Roman Empire*, a beautifully conceived and mellifluously written history in the tradition of Gibbon.

We are inclined to jest at an empire that was so notoriously neither holy nor Roman nor an empire, but it represented the urge in man for some kind of a world rule — a United Nations, if you will — a feeling of Christians, derived perhaps even from pagan Rome, that the kingdom of God, to be valid, had to be a single, a universal one. Bryce's treatise on the practical results of this wholly impracticable concept provides a fascinating new light on the vagaries of European history.

He sees the coronation of Charlemagne in 800 as a turning

point in the evolution of modern Europe. "From that chair the Pope now rose, as the reading of the Gospel ended, advanced to where Charles — who had exchanged his simple Frankish dress for the sandals and chlamys of a Roman patrician — knelt in prayer by the high altar, and in the sight of all he placed upon the brow of the barbarian chieftain the diadem of the Caesars." Charles was held to be the legitimate successor, not of Romulus Augustulus, the so-called last of the emperors of the West, who had been forced to abdicate in 476, but of Constantine VI, the emperor of the East, and theoretically of the world, who had been lawlessly dethroned by his usurping mother, Irene, in 792. Thus Charlemagne, in creating the Holy Empire, meant to close the gap between himself and the great Augustus! Constantinople, after that, was in the eyes of Europe a usurping capital, until its deserved eclipse in 1454. But the "true" empire of God lasted until Napoleon dissolved it in 1806. And even then the conquering Corsican continued it in a fashion by calling himself an emperor and his son the king of Rome.

Henry James met Bryce at this time. While conceding that he talked well and was "distinctly able," he noted that Bryce possessed three conflicting dispositions — literature, law and politics — and "had not made a complete thing of any one of them." James saw him as belonging to the class of "young doctrinaire radicals who don't take the popular heart and seem booked to remain out of things."

Bryce managed to support himself in London with the sales of his treatise, by writing articles and occasional briefs, and with the salary that came to him as regius professor of civil law at Oxford, a sinecure that required him only to make a speech in Latin at the presentation of an honorary degree. It is always difficult to determine what money the great Victorians lived on, because the contemporary two-volume "life and letters," with its expensive plates of pompous portraits protected by onion paper, never incurred the charge of poor taste by discussing money. However, life in London was not expensive for a bachelor, and Bryce did not have to marry his security until 1889, when he was fifty-one. His wife, the former Marion Ashton of Manchester, then brought him a fortune derived from cotton spinning, a London apartment at Buckingham Gate and a country estate in Sussex.

As Bryce was all his life a determined traveller and explorer, it would have been surprising if he had not come to the United States. He was a democrat, and here was democracy; he was an educationalist, and where else would he have found public education carried out on such a scale? He paid his first visit to our shores in 1870 at the age of thirty-two, and in the words of his biographer, Herbert A. Fisher, "here he found great and unaffected simplicity, an engaging spirit of equality and a quickening sense of hopefulness, as inspiring as the dry, nimble air and the stainless blue sky of an American Fall . . . He fell in love with the United States; it was almost a case of love at first sight."

A second visit, in 1881, took him to the Pacific and Southern states. A third, in 1883, took him to the Northwest and the Hawaiian Islands. It was during the third visit that the idea of *The American Commonwealth* took root.

Bryce's method of research was constant inquiry. Waiters in hotels were asked how they spent their savings; conductors on trains, how they enforced nonsmoking rules; university men, lawyers, politicians and captains of industry were quizzed on the details of their work and recreation. Nothing seemed to escape his notice, from the number of advertisements of soothsayers in a San Francisco newspaper to the mortgage interest rates in Walla Walla.

Bryce was a friendly man and a good mixer, and Americans, many of whom still had a chip on their shoulder about British snobbishness, found his infinite curiosity about, and his obvious admiration for, their country endearing.

He began to write his great book after the third trip, but his time was far from free. In 1880 he was elected to Parliament as a Liberal. His career in the House of Commons, however, was not a noted success. He was too professorial. As Fisher pointed out, Bryce, in a speech against Irish coercion, would lay down the principle that one democratic community could never govern another democratic community by force. Then it would occur to him that Switzerland and Sonderbund might constitute an exception to his rule, and he would bore the House by explaining in detail why his cited exception was really not apposite to the issue. But he cared only for the truth. As William James put it, to Bryce all facts were born free and equal.

In 1886 Prime Minister Gladstone appointed him undersecretary for foreign affairs and, in 1892, chancellor of the Duchy of Lancaster. The latter was a cabinet sinecure that enabled Gladstone to utilize Bryce's full energies in drafting the Home Rule bill for Ireland. In 1894 he became president of the Board of Trade in Lord Rosebery's cabinet, and in 1906 chief secretary for Ireland. It should be noted that if he bored fellow members of Parliament, even in an age of notable loquacity, his was never the dullness associated with mossbacks. He was always a liberal: pro-Irish, pro-American, Pro-Armenian, even pro-Boer. Only about women's suffrage did he remain a conservative. His chivalrous, lacey-valentine concept of the pure, ideal woman who must never be sullied by the ballot kept him to the end in male chauvinist ranks, where he did not otherwise belong.

The defeat of the Home Rule bill threw the Liberal Party into opposition, and Bryce was able at last to devote the bulk of his time to writing *The American Commonwealth*, which was finally published in 1888.

His design in these three volumes was nothing less than to describe the government of the United States and of the several states, their constitutions, the political parties and the ideas, temper and habits of the "sovereign people." In later editions he added chapters on new subjects, such as the latest phase of immigration, foreign policy, industrial expansion, the future of the Negro, and particular political events, which was not altogether a happy idea. The book is too vast a compendium of facts and opinions to be subject to amendment. It has to be an America caught in a point of time, 1888, and left there.

His appreciation of the American experiment in constitutional government was so profound, and his affection for the American people so evident, that even his severest criticisms of the political system were taken in good part on our side of the Atlantic. He understood the purpose of our system of checks and balances, but he was always conscious of what we paid for it.

The presidency, for example, did not appeal to our men of greatest talent. The president did not address the legislature, as did the British prime minister, nor could he submit bills. His appointments and treaties were subject to a jealously guarded power of approval by the Senate. The politicians who nominated him preferred a good candidate to a good chief executive. If elected, he had no need of great intellectual gifts; his job was like that of a manager of a railway or a chairman of a commercial company. So long as he was honest and made the right appointments, he could get by.

The modern reader may be amused by Bryce's downgrading of the White House, but he himself pointed out what most differentiated his time from our own: in his we had no national deficit and no threatening neighbors. Americans could afford a long succession of mediocre leaders.

Of the two houses of Congress, Bryce found the Senate the more important. He even believed that its essential function was to act as a restraint to the larger and less disciplined House of Representatives. But he thought that Congress was hampered in having imperfect powers over the president, just as the president was hampered in having no initiative in Congress. The result was that the nation did not know where to fix responsibility for misfeasance or neglect. Friction had resulted in a loss of force. By relieving the administration of the duty of legislative sessions and by seeking to make members of Congress independent of the executive branch, the founding fathers had condemned the latter to be "architects without science, critics without experience, censors without responsibility."

Bryce made the further point that all the carefully devised machinery of the Constitution had done little to solve the problem of slavery or to avert the Civil War, and he noted that President Lincoln had had to free himself from constitutional shackles to bring that conflict to a successful conclusion. Yet as soon as it was over, the reign of legality had returned. A people capable of such adjustments, Bryce concluded, "can work any constitution," but they should never lose sight of the faults of their political machinery.

Coming now to the two great political parties, Bryce observed that Europeans could never make out that they had any distinctive tenets. But he found their differences in their attitudes towards the salient feature of the Constitution: its effort to establish an equipoise between the force that would carry the planet states off into space and the force that would draw them back into their orbit of the sun of national government. He saw the Democrats as favoring states' rights, and the Republicans, who had inherited the authoritarianism of the Puritans, as supporting stronger federal powers. In our day it would appear to be just the reverse.

Bryce was properly shocked by the corruption of political machines, particularly in the big cities. When he attended a state convention in Rochester, New York, he noted that the important decisions had been taken before the public proceedings. All that the man in the gallery could observe was "a tremendous coming and going and chattering and clattering of crowds of men who looked at once sordid and flashy, faces shrewd but mean and sometimes brutal . . ."

In the last analysis he concluded that the system of checks and balances had to be monitored by public opinion. It was that opinion, operating with a force unknown in any European country, which really kept America going. But Bryce's final warning was that our Constitution was not really being tested by world events in the 1880s. The ship of state was still "sailing upon a summer sea."

The success of *The American Commonwealth* on both sides of the Atlantic and its many subsequent editions gave Bryce an immense following in the United States, but it was not for two decades after its first publication that, in 1907, he was finally appointed the British ambassador. His friendship with Theodore Roosevelt was undoubtedly a factor in this appointment. The two men had much in common: scholarship, politics, exploration and the vigorous life.

Roosevelt's daughter Ethel Derby once told me that her family had found Bryce prolix and tedious. But I doubt that her father shared that view. Did there not have to be a real congeniality between two such danger-defying men? Roosevelt, even as president, would ascend a rock face two hundred feet high in Rock Creek Park and once crossed an incomplete suspension bridge, swinging himself from girder to girder by his arms, with certain death the penalty of a fall. Bryce, on the edge of the great crater Kilauea, in Hawaii, slipped through a fissure obscured by brushwood and would have plunged to a fiery death in the bowels of the volcano had he not managed to catch hold of a small shrub on the side and slowly work his way back to the surface. His ascents included Mauna Loa in Hawaii, Machache in Basutoland, Myogisan in Japan and Ararat in Armenia.

Bryce's ambassadorship, which lasted until 1913, was outstandingly successful, but he suffered three major disappointments. A proposed reciprocal tariff reduction between Canada and the United States was scuttled because of fear in Ottawa that Canada might be absorbed into the American economy. Bryce, who had to exercise great tact, because the Canadians had then no diplomatic representative in Washington, nonetheless fell between two stools, being accused in Ottawa of thinking only of the British Empire and criticized in the House of Commons for fostering divisiveness between Britain and her colony.

A second disappointment came when the Senate eviscerated a proposed arbitration agreement between the United States and Britain by excluding from it such essential subjects as aliens, boundaries and the Monroe Doctrine. And finally Bryce was unsuccessful in opposing the Panama Canal bill, which exempted American ships from tolls, in flagrant contravention of the Hay-Pauncefote Treaty. He was vindicated, however, after his return to England, when this bill was repealed at the request of President Wilson in 1914.

But all these setbacks were as nothing compared with Bryce's triumphs in public relations. He was invited to speak everywhere and covered with honorary degrees. A large part of his years as ambassador was spent in travelling about the

United States. Because his intimacy had been with Republican Presidents Roosevelt and Taft, and because he was over seventy years of age, he was replaced in 1913 by Sir Cecil Spring-Rice, who was to play a major role in bringing the United States into alliance with Britain in World War I.

During the war Bryce headed a committee to investigate German atrocities in Belgium. This was his last important public work. He died in 1922. To the very end he continued to be engaged in his voluminous reading and wide correspondence in an effort simply to understand the whole world.

WALTER PATER

❧   ❧   ❧

A S LITERARY LIVES GO, that of Walter Pater (1839–1894) was probably as literary as a life can be. Indeed, some modern critics seem to question the fact that he had any life at all. Because his manner was reserved, because he led for so many years the cloistered life of an Oxford don, because he never married and lived with two maiden sisters, because he wrote exquisite prose and professed to find his greatest rapture in the contemplation of beautiful things, he is treated with considerable condescencion as a man to whom nothing of significance ever happened. "Faint, pale, embarrassed, exquisite Pater!" Henry James called him. Yet how did his external life really differ from James's except for a thousand and one dinner parties?

How much, indeed, did it differ from the lives of half of his academic critics, except for the occasional fondlings of a spouse? One would think, to read them, that their own existences had been full of tiger hunts or polar explorations. Pater taught classes, had private sessions with students, gave public lectures and travelled widely in Europe, preferring stiff hikes to railway trips. Later in his life he established a household in London and was a frequent guest at literary gatherings. A premature death at age fifty-five from heart failure put a sudden end to what had been a physically active life.

Such were the things that he did. But what *didn't* he do? That is the great thing to us moderns. Well, he didn't, so far as one can tell, give any physical outlet to his sexual urges, although there is clear evidence in his writing that he was strongly attracted to young men. In our society homosexuality is widely accepted — totally so in circles of any sophistication — but any sort of sexual inhibition is still regarded as faintly derisory. The sly peeker who dares not touch is the butt of crude jokes. It doesn't matter what his temptation is so long as he gives in to it. Life without orgasm is less than a half life. Perhaps Pater himself contributed to this attitude when he replied to the question of what he would choose to be if he couldn't be a human: "A carp swimming forever in the green waters of a royal chateau."

We don't know why Pater remained chaste, or even, for that matter, whether he really did so. He may have been disgusted by the idea of physical sex, particularly among men; there is a passage in *Marius the Epicurean*, quite without tangible relation to the rest of the novel, describing the hero's horror at the sight of copulating serpents. He may have deemed it a sin; that was certainly the majority view in his day. He may have believed, as implied in *Marius*, that chastity conserved energy vital to the powers of the imagination and the appreciation of beauty in art and nature. Or he may simply have dreaded the social stigma that would follow the discovery of an illicit love affair. Consider what happened to Oscar Wilde! My own theory is that he thought of physical love as beautiful only when it involved two beautiful beings and that his ugliness barred him from desecrating an act designed for gods. "I would give ten years of my life to be handsome," he once said.

But what did it really matter to the artist in him? How many minutes in how many years of an average life are spent in sexual acts? Pater had all the thoughts and feelings of another man. I doubt there would have been a line changed in *Marius* had his two little greenish-white rooms in Brasenose College, with their delicate line etchings, been the scene of student seductions.

Earlier critics of Pater, his contemporaries, saw him not so much as a man of inaction as one who was preaching a doctrine dangerous to youth. It showed how vulnerable they deemed their own establishment. If "to burn with a gem-like flame" as one wandered through the galleries of the Louvre or the Uffizi, if to derive the fullest possible delight from the contemplation of the *Mona Lisa* or Botticelli's *Birth of Venus* was to shake the Church of England or the Empire, then those institutions were indeed in danger. For Pater was no rebel; indeed, he was a model citizen. He broke no law; he paid his bills; he was a considerate neighbor and a good brother. If he took no particular interest in politics or in public causes, it was probably because the status quo suited him very well. He needed law and order to pursue his own quiet way of life and study, and Victorian England provided him with plenty of both. I suspect that, like the little bookbinder in Henry James's *The Princess Casamassima*, he would have thought the social improvements brought on by a revolution inadequate compensation for the beautiful objects that its violence might destroy, but I can perfectly see him, in a Britain occupied by an enemy army, joining the underground.

Today there is a new school of thought about Pater: that he was one of those who made English literature European and set it on its antithetical and antinomian course. As Denis Donoghue puts it in his *Walter Pater*, his subject represents the perfection of standing aside. Pater, along with Swinburne, Rossetti, Beardsley, Wilde and Yeats,

> made themselves an 'adversary' life when official life was deemed to be bourgeois, Protestant, imperial, male and heterosexual. They did not dissent from these values in every particular, but they felt no loyalty to the consensus that these values implied. Pater simply hoped to take the harm out of these attitudes by making them doubt themselves.

Although I agree entirely that Pater did not for a minute believe that a man should be ruled in his heart or mind by the touted values of the majority — or of the social establishment that always purports to speak for the majority — I fail to see why that makes him such a pioneer among modernists. It seems to me that he simply displayed the sensitivity and independence that must inhabit the soul of any fine artist. Of course, there are some great writers, like Pierre Corneille, for example, who happened to go along with the patriotic and military values of their era, but Corneille was essentially quite as independent as Pater. He *chose* to exalt the *gloire* of the Sun King; he honestly believed in it. Sympathy or lack of sympathy with the slogans of the day has little to do with the artist at work on the only thing he really cares about: his art.

And Donoghue, I maintain, again goes too far when he says that Pater lived out of the world, not only in his life but in his fiction. He concludes about Pater the novelist:

> And while he can imagine what it would be like to hold an idea, he can't imagine any consequences of holding it, the difference it would make. In his sense of the world at large it would make no difference, because he gives this

world such tenuous acknowledgement. In the life within, it makes only the difference between having an idea and not having one.

Finally, Donoghue accuses Pater of reneging on the philosophy of art for art's sake with which Donoghue has arbitrarily endowed him, of making the "wretched concession" that good art depends on its form, but that great art depends on its matter. The passage that evokes this accusation is from Pater's essay "Style":

> Given the conclusions I have tried to explain as constituting good art; — then if it be devoted further to the increase of men's happiness, to the redemption of the oppressed, or the enlargement of our sympathies with each other, or to such presentment of new or old truth about ourselves and our relation to the world as may ennoble and fortify us in our sojourn here, or immediately, as with Dante, to the glory of God, it will be also great art.

I don't regard this as a "wretched concession"; I deem it the simple statement of Pater's lifelong credo. Nor does it make me wince, fulsome as it may sound to a modern ear. I maintain impenitently that the hero of *Marius the Epicurean* dies a martyr's death at the end of his story as a direct consequence of "holding an idea."

Marius has devoted his youth to the intellectual search of a philosophy of life that will bring him the highest satisfaction. He is never attracted to mere bodily pleasures; the brand of epicureanism that he studies has nothing to do with wine, women and song. There has always to be a moral aspect in each new ideology that he tests for himself. The stern old religion of Numa of his boyhood was not one to take or leave lightly; "it seemed to involve certain heavy demands on him," as an aristocrat, a leader and a son. And when he visited the hospital of Aesculapius he learned "the refined and sacred happiness of a life spent in the relieving of pain."

The epicurean principles that he imbibed in early manhood would indeed seem to be those ascribed to Pater by Donoghue, but it must be remembered that this was only the midpoint of Marius's intellectual journey:

> To keep the eye clear by a sort of exquisite personal alacrity and cleanliness, extending even to his dwelling place; to discriminate, ever more and more fastidiously, select form and colour in things from what was less select; to meditate much on beautiful visible objects, on objects, more especially, connected with the period of youth — on children at play in the morning, the trees in early spring, on young animals, on the fashions and amusements of young men; to keep ever by him if it were but a single choice flower, a graceful animal or sea shell, as a token and representative of the whole kingdom of such things; to avoid jealously, on his way through the world, everything repugnant to sight . . . such were in brief outline the duties recognized, the rights demanded in this new formula of life.

But all this changes when he enters the employ of the stoic emperor, Marcus Aurelius, and learns to admire the orderly, disciplined life of that virtuous man who was able to combine scholastic and philosophic studies with the efficient and just administration of a vast empire. Yet the great lesson that the emperor taught Marius was not one that he intended. It was that his habit of reading learned tracts while occupying the imperial box at the games to distract his attention from the slaughter below did not excuse him from his responsibility to the wretched animals and gladiators.

> There was something in a tolerance such as this, in the bare fact that he could sit patiently through a scene like this, which seemed to Marius to mark Aurelius as his inferior now and forever on the question of righteousness; to set them on opposite sides, in some great conflict, of which that difference was but a single presentment. Due, in whatever proportions, to the abstract principles he had formulated for himself, or in spite of them, there was the loyal conscience within him, deciding, judging himself and everyone else with a wonderful sort of authority: — You ought, methinks, to be something quite different from what you are; here! and here!

How Pater could state the moral imperative more strongly, I don't know. Marius is now ready for Christianity, to which he is introduced by the severe but serene centurion Cornelius. In some of Pater's most beautiful passages he describes the pure and simple life (as he sees it) of the second-century members of that new and still persecuted sect, before the advent of doctrinal conflicts and quibbling heresies. Marius is not actually converted, but when he and Cornelius are arrested for their supposed involvement in a local earthquake blamed on the Christians, Marius, by a ruse of which his righteous friend is totally unaware, contrives to free him to seek counsel in Rome while he himself is left to die of fever aggravated by the rough marches of the guards.

> In one quarter of an hour, under a sudden, incontrollable impulse, hardly weighing what he did, almost as a matter

of course and as lightly as one hires a bed for one's night's rest on a journey, Marius had taken on himself all the heavy risk of the position in which Cornelius had then been . . . He had delivered his brother, after the manner he had sometimes vaguely anticipated as a kind of distinction in his destiny.

Marius may not have been confirmed by the rites of the church; he may not even have been ready for that; but the Christians who gather at his bedside chant, *"Abi, abi, anima christiana."* However "modern" Pater may be, his Marius seems closer to Sidney Carton than to Dorian Gray.

Morals, indeed, are to be found in all of Pater's fiction; they are not so much repudiated by his style as intrinsic in it. Sebastian Van Storck, in his eponymous tale, a handsome and rich young seventeenth-century Dutchman, the most eligible bachelor of Haarlem, has no interest in his privileges or in the life of pleasure around him. His thoughts dwell on the seeming infinity of the neighboring sea; he seems "in love with death, preferring winter to summer, finding only a tranquillizing influence in the thought of the earth beneath our feet cooling down forever from its old cosmic heat." The brief spirit of life itself is to him only "as the pallid arctic sun, disclosing itself over the dead level of a glacial, barren and absolutely lonely sea." What he forces himself to admire is the void, the tabula rasa to which all the energies of man and nature were settling.

The prose in which Pater describes Van Storck's "dark fanaticism" is for me quite the equal of his famous passage on the *Mona Lisa* in his essay about Leonardo, but its eeriness makes it less popular. In the end, Van Storck, having chosen to remain in a cottage by the sea despite the imminent danger of a break in the dam, is drowned in the subsequent flood, but he is drowned in a successful effort to save a child. The moral is as pointed as in the old rhyme of William Camden:

Betwixt the stirrup and the ground
Mercy I asked; mercy I found.

In "A Prince of Court Painters" the essential despondency in the character of Antoine Watteau is seen as the result of the division in his heart and mind between the pull of the simple and innocent Flemish family background in which he was raised and the attraction of the brilliant frivolities of French court life.

Anthony Watteau reproduces that gallant world, those patched and powdered ladies and fine cavaliers, so much to its own satisfaction, partly because he despises it; if this be a possible condition of excellent artistic production. People talk of a new era now dawning upon the world, of fraternity, liberty, humanity . . . Himself really of the old time — that serious old time which is passing away, the impress of which he carries on his physiognomy — he dignifies, by what in him is neither more nor less than a profound melancholy, the essential insignificance of what he *wills* to touch in all that, transforming its mere pettiness into grace.

The storm is always brooding through the massy splendor of the trees in his paintings of garden fêtes; the trees themselves "would hardly last another generation."

The "ideas" held by Watteau may have no direct "consequences," but their indirect consequence is the entire personality of the painter. He is never seen as a happy man, although some of his despondency can be attributed to ill health; he is doomed to be forever seeking something that cannot be found in this world. He is the victim of a deep ambivalence between the world of his childhood and the world he wishes to conquer. He cannot reconcile himself to the love of the narrator, who is too simple a Flemish woman to be his consort in Paris; he cannot even treat her brother decently when the latter comes to work for him. The narrator thinks "he would have been happier had he remained obscure in Valenciennes." The reader knows better.

In "Emerald Uthwart" an idea held by two characters has actually a catastrophic consequence. Here the hero and his best friend, officers in a war in Flanders, disobey orders to effect a daring raid into enemy territory to recover a captured standard, and return to discover that their company has been ordered into action in their absence. They are court-martialed and sentenced to be shot, but the penalty is remitted to a dishonorable discharge in Emerald's case, and he returns to his family home in Sussex to die of melancholy aggravated by an old war wound. I suppose, without being at all sure, that Emerald's fatal idea was spawned by a passionate romanticism born in the ancient and beautiful halls of the cathedral school he attended in Canterbury and in his lonely and contemplative childhood on the lovely grounds of the family farm. Such high thoughts may have brought him into collision with a society that depends on discipline and obedience: the poet against the establishment.

Or maybe what Donoghue says about *Marius* is true of "Emerald Uthwart," that the best thing that can be said of it is that it is an achievement of style. He adds: "But style is nearly all that the literature from Pater to Wallace Stevens claims to achieve; it must not be deemed to count for nothing. It counts for a distinctive possibility of living, mostly by ruses, by circumventing the standard terms which modern societies offer as the means of living."

But I repeat that I believe that Pater meant what he said: that great art should ennoble and fortify us on our sojourn on earth, and I like the fact that he, the great stylist, wasn't afraid to sound corny.

JOHN WALTER CROSS

*(as Lytton Strachey
might have conceived him)*

❧ ❧ ❧

JOHN WALTER CROSS (1840–1924), the widower of George
Eliot and the editor of her letters and journal ("three
volumes of reticence," according to W. E. Gladstone), first
met the subject of his life's worship in 1869 in the Pamphili
Gardens in Rome, where the great author and her husband
in all but name, George H. Lewes, were engaged, in their
usual relentless fashion, and despite the ever present plague
of headaches and drooping health, in the duties of sightseeing. Cross had met Lewes two years before and, like
everyone else, had been impressed by his wit and broad
knowledge. But the great thing about him, of course, was his
relationship to the English sybil whose fiction was so passionately admired by Cross, as well as by his widowed mother
and maiden sisters. Lewes himself — one had to face it —
was ugly, almost ape-like, manoeuvering, insinuating, saying
too many things in too many languages, smilingly agree-
ably — oh, yes — but with a way of leaving one the unex-
pected depositary of an unsought obligation to do some little
favor for him. In short, not quite a gentleman. Had he not
once even been an actor?

But *she*! The author of *Middlemarch* and *Romola*! The most

famous woman of the age, if one excepted the queen and
Florence Nightingale! Cross was as enraptured by her looks as
his friend Henry James, who had written to his father in
America: "She is magnificently ugly, deliciously hideous. She
had a low forehead, a dull grey eye, a vast pendulous nose, a
huge mouth full of uneven teeth and a chin and jawbone *qui
n'en finissent pas* . . . Now in this vast ugliness resides a most
powerful beauty which in a very few minutes steals forth and
charms the mind, so that you end as I have ended, in falling
in love with her." And indeed Cross *did* fall in love with her,
and much less figuratively than had the author of *Portrait of a
Lady*; the twenty-one years between their ages seemed only
the proper distance between the priestess and the acolyte.

The Leweses' visit to Weybridge, home of the Crosses,
when both families were back in England, cemented the
friendship. As Cross was later to write: "Sympathetic feelings
were strong enough to overleap the barrier (often hard to
pass) which separates acquaintanceship from friendship. A
day did the work of years. Our visitors had come to the house
as acquaintances; they left it as lifelong friends."

Cross hoped that there would be things he could do for his
new idol. There were. Lewes sought his advice on invest-
ments, for Cross was a successful banker in London, and used
his free services as a broker in seeking out and purchasing a
country seat. George Eliot enjoyed his affability, his admiration, his availability. If he was not her intellectual equal, how
many men were? He listened well, and he remembered
everything she said. Soon she was writing him, on his return
from a business trip: "What a comfort that you are at home
again and well! The sense of your long nearness has been so
long missing to us that we had begun to take up with life as
inevitably a little less cheerful than we remembered it to have

been formerly . . . Let us comfort each other while it is day, for the night cometh." And now she was calling him her dear "nephew."

Still, there was something that worried this handsome, stalwart, conscientious and conservative young Britisher. Mrs. Lewes might call herself that, but she indubitably was not. She was still Miss Evans, and Lewes's legal spouse, however depraved and shameless, was still very much alive. Indeed, she was producing child after child by Lewes's own publishing partner, and Lewes was weak enough to support these brats with the royalties of George Eliot's masterpieces! Would a gentleman do that? And although great men called on the Leweses, great men's wives did not always accompany them. Princess Louise, a sculptor, might mold a likeness of the novelist; a presentation to her royal mother (though Victoria adored *The Mill on the Floss*) would have been unthinkable. Cross's mother, a woman of broad views, had explained to her son that George Eliot's "marriage" was a holier and more serious relationship than many altar-blessed unions, and he accepted the judgment of his adored parent, but it was still troubling.

He himself was a strictly virtuous young man. Should he marry, he wished to be as pure as the bride who would come to him without a stain. At Rugby he had turned contemptuously away from any boy who suggested that they engage in unnatural acts. Indeed, he had shown a horror as of hell fire. The fact that any such lewd proposition should have left him panting and exhausted from a sick temptation showed how powerful the devil was. And now that he had reached an age where his sisters were beginning to make sly references to any eligible maiden in their society as a possible "in-law," he found himself wondering whether behind the blinking eyes and giggles of presentable virgins there might not lurk the seed of the kind of inclination that had turned Guinevere from her matchless husband to Lancelot. For Johnny Cross dearly loved the *Idylls of the King*. He had been much upset when the all-knowing, all-judging Eliot had appeared to slight them and relieved when she had had the kindness to pen him an explanatory note.

I did not mean to say Amen when the Idylls of the King seemed to be judged rather *de haut en bas*. I only meant that I should value for my own mind *In Memoriam* as the chief of the larger works, and that while I feel exquisite beauty in passages scattered through the Idylls, I must judge some smaller wholes among the lyrics as the works most decisive of Tennyson's high place among the immortals.

She always made everything right!

Cross, who was now present at many of the social gatherings at the Leweses', gives us this picture of the hostess:

When the drawing-room door opened, a first glance revealed her always in the same low arm-chair at the left hand side of the fire. On entering the visitor's eye was at once arrested by the massive head. The abundant hair, streaked with grey now, was draped with lace, arranged mantilla-fashion, coming to a point at the top of the forehead. If she were engaged in conversation, her body was usually bent forward with eager, anxious desire to get as close as possible to the person with whom she talked. She had a great dislike of raising her voice and often became so totally absorbed in conversation, that the announcement of an incoming visitor sometimes failed to attract her attention; but the moment the eyes were lifted up, and recognized a friend, they smiled a rare welcome — sincere, cordial, grave — a welcome that was felt to come straight from the heart.

But Cross did not allow her to confine herself to parlor life. He induced her to play tennis and even badminton!

In 1878 the two families were drawn even closer by the fatal illnesses of Mrs. Cross and Lewes. Death came to both in the same week. "From this time forward I saw George Eliot constantly," wrote Cross. Trying to distract his mind from his own grief, he took up reading Dante. "Oh, I must read that with you," George Eliot exclaimed. And so it was. "In the following twelve months we read through the Inferno and the Paradisio together, not in a dilettante way, but with minute and careful examination of the construction of every sentence . . . The divine poet took us into a new world."

Eliot, however, was not one to overlook the fact that she had long preceded her young friend into that world, or that he could inhabit it on anything like equal terms with herself. She was capable, like a benevolent governess, of pulling her pupil up short with a reminder that it was his heart rather than his mind that provided her solace:

Through everything else, dear tender one, there is the blessing of trusting in thy goodness. Thou dost not know anything of verbs Hiphil or Hophal or the history of metaphysics or the position of Kepel in science, but thou knowest best things of another sort, such as belong to the manly heart — secrets of lovingness and rectitude. O I am flattering. Consider what thou wast a little time ago in pantaloons.

But he took everything in just the spirit in which it was intended. Their association grew steadily deeper.

As the year went on George Eliot began to see all her old friends again. But her life was nonetheless a life of heart-loneliness. Accustomed as she had been for so many years to solitude *à deux*, the want of close companionship continued to be very bitterly felt. She was in the habit of going with me very frequently to the National Gallery, and other exhibitions of pictures, to the British Museum sculptures, and to South Kensington. This constant association engrossed me completely, and was a new interest to her. A bond of mutual dependence had been formed between us.

At this point in such a relationship between any man and woman — even if she be a poorish sixty and he a blooming forty — there is bound to be some talk of marriage, even jestingly. Cross was beginning to see his mission in life as the nurture and protection of England's first literary genius. She had not published a novel since *Daniel Deronda*, four years back. Might she not still exceed even such a masterpiece as *Middlemarch*? With rest, with moderate travel, with a steady aide always at her side to regulate the household and the influx of eager visitors, might not the old serenity be restored? Perhaps the badminton had been a mite too much.

Marriage? Well, why not? It would never do even to hint to Mrs. Lewes that the ceremony would make her a *legal* Mrs. Cross, but might it not still be his privilege — his august privilege — at least in the eyes of such of her devoted following as were faithful members of the Church of England to bring the perhaps too freely thinking translator of Strauss's *Life of Jesus* into the ranks of orthodox brides?

"But no, dear Johnny," one can almost hear her near whisper, "some dear young creature is what a man like you requires. If this old body of mine should ever take on another mate, it would have to be a union chaste as snow."

"Johnny," she was sure, would never hear of such a match. What? He *would*? It was actually what he himself had been thinking of daring to propose — but oh, so reverently, so respectfully, of course? One can imagine the grave headshake with which *this* would have been greeted. But the headshake did not have to mean that it would not be at least considered.

His third proposal was accepted, and they were married on May 6, 1880, in Saint George's on Hanover Square in London. Charles Lewes gave his stepmother away, and after the ceremony the bride and groom signed new wills (the marriage was not to disturb the former testamentary plans of either party) and set out for Dover.

Isaac Evans, Eliot's brother and the prototype of Tom Tulliver in *The Mill on the Floss*, who had not communicated with his sister since her elopement with Lewes, now wrote to congratulate the redeemed sinner. Eliot in her cool reply seemed to wish him to know that she had not entrapped a younger man or deprived him of a more suitable match for his age. "The only point to be regretted in our marriage is that I am much older than he, but his affection has made him choose this lot of caring for me rather than any other of the various lots open to him."

The long leisurely honeymoon proceeded as planned: from Dover to Paris to Grenoble to Milan to Verona. Eliot flourished; she was enchanted by the speed of her recovery from old ailments and the renewal of her strength. Her enthusiasm for exhaustive sightseeing returned. She wrote glowingly to Charles Lewes:

> But marriage has seemed to restore me to my old health. I was getting hard, and if I had decided differently, I think I should have become very selfish. To feel daily the loveliness of a nature close to me, and to feel grateful for it, is the fountain of tenderness and strength to endure. Glorious weather always, and I am very well — quite amazingly able to go through fatigue.

And she was equally exultant in her letters to Cross's sister:

> Our life since we wrote to you has been a chapter of delights — Grenoble — Grande Chartreuse — Chambéry — a paradisiacal walk to Les Charmettes — roses gathered in Jean-Jacque's garden — Mont Cenis Tunnel, and the emergence into Italian sunshine. Milan, comfortable *appartement*, delicious privacy and great minds condescending to relax themselves!

And then in Venice it all blew up. John Cross jumped from their hotel suite into the Grand Canal and had to be fished out by gondoliers.

The Victorian morality first-aid kit was rushed to the scene. Here is how Cross described what had happened. He complained that their bedroom windows opened on the great drain of the Grand Canal:

> The effect of this continual bad air, and the complete and sudden deprivation of all bodily exercise made me thoroughly ill. As soon as I could be moved we left Venice, on the 23rd of June, and went to Innsbruck where we stayed

for a week, and in the change to the pure sweet mountain air I soon regained strength.

Eliot confirmed this in a letter to a friend, but hinted at earlier anxieties:

> Mr. Cross had a sharp but brief attack in Venice, due to the unsanitary influences of that wondrous city, in the later weeks of June. We stayed a little too long there, with a continuous sirocco blowing, and bad smells under the windows of the hotel; and these conditions found him a little below par from the long protracted anxiety before our marriage.

What really happened? Strong men don't jump out of windows because of siroccos. It had to be suicidal; the ridiculous prospect of being fished out alive would have been worse than death to a man like Cross. There were later allegations of nervous depression and insanity in the Cross family, but those are notoriously recurrent ailments, and there is no record of repetition in the forty-four ensuing years of Cross's serenely uneventful life. Everything points to a sexual embarrassment; consummation was not an infrequent problem in Victorian marriages; the Thomas Carlyles and the John Ruskins come easily to mind.

Is it not possible that George Eliot, feeling so much stronger as the honeymoon happily progressed, and enraptured by the assiduous devotion of her new travelling companion, may, in romantic Venice, have decided to offer her husband what she presumed he had been too delicate — too faithful to his pledge — to demand as his right? Ah, if he really loved her as he professed . . . !

And then — horror! Poor Cross is faced with the afflicting

sight of a naked, skinny, ill old woman. He has brought England's sybil to this pass, humiliating her and himself beyond redemption! What can he do but rush for the window?

Yet he was rescued and cured to return with his bride to England and live in apparent peace and happiness for the few remaining months of her life. Again, what happened? Isn't it possible that she behaved with prompt kindness and wisdom? That she convinced him that she should have never deviated from her original concept of a *mariage blanc*, that she hadn't really wanted to, that it had just been her silly notion that she owed it to him, that she wanted nothing so much as to get back to where they had been, which had been just about heaven? And surely she had not been a great novelist for nothing. John had been convinced; he had hardly the alternative not to be.

After Eliot's sudden death in the same year John never married again. Indeed, his life became almost invisible. But he did weave together his wife's many letters and journals into a kind of autobiography, with brief notes of his own to provide the whole with a glaze of benevolent interpretation.

There is something almost heroic about this kind of Victorian gloss. Take, for example, how Cross deals with Charles and Caroline Bray, early and intimate friends of his wife. We now know that the Brays had what is called an open marriage, of which Eliot was well aware. Caroline had, so far as we know, only a single lover, Edward Henry Noel, a married man with a consumptive wife and three children, related, appropriately, to Byron, but Charles, the Don Juan of his neighborhood, sired six children on the Brays' cook, one of whom he actually persuaded his wife to adopt. It is quite possible that he had an affair with the young Mary Ann Evans (George Eliot), and if so, Caroline surely knew all about it. How did John Cross deal with this situation? Very simply. He wrote that his wife turned to Mrs. Bray "when she is in pain or trouble, and wants affectionate companionship; with Mr. Bray she quarrels, and the humorous side of her nature is brought out. Every good story goes to him with a certainty that it will be appreciated. With all three it is a beautiful and consistent friendship, running like a thread through the woof of the coming thirty-eight years."

Any more questions?

The Two Literary Lives
of HENRY JAMES:
American and English

۶⵿ٔ ۶⵿ٔ ۶⵿ٔ

H ENRY JAMES published *The American Scene* in 1907, when
he was sixty-four, to record his impressions of his native
land revisited, after an absence of two decades, in a year-long
tour from coast to coast in 1904–1905. He had planned, and
even negotiated for, the book before he left England; he had
every intention of creating what it indeed became: a significant work of art. As he wrote to his publishers early in the
trip, and only half-humorously (such are our real meanings!):
"I am moved inwardly to believe that I shall not only be able
to write the best book of social and pictorial and, as it were,
human observation, but one of the best — or why 'drag' in
one *of*, why not say frankly *the* best? — ever devoted to any
country at all."

He would have called the book *The Return of the Native*
had not Hardy pre-empted the title. And also, as originally
planned, the book would not have been simply the observations of a former domiciliary. The second part, never written, would have included the author's visits to Indianapolis,
Chicago, Saint Louis and California, places where he had
never before set foot. And even in the first part, he describes
his travels to the hitherto unvisited North Carolina, Charleston and Florida. The bulk of the book, however, deals with

the America in which he had spent most of the first forty years of his life: New York and New England; and for these chapters the Hardy title would have been appropriate. They are what differentiate *The American Scene* from his many travel books and essays and bring it closer to the greatest fiction of his rich late style. There is nothing finer in all his work than the extraordinary double vision afforded us of an idyllic earlier America supplanted by a culture of mightier force and perhaps superior vigor, but always at the price of an excess of what he liked to call "rush and huddle." Even in the shadow of the statue of such a serene thinker as Ralph Waldo Emerson, James was aware of the constantly shouted urban warning: "Step lively!"

In the few places where he had no memories around which to embroider the threads of his double theme, James could sound fretful, even trivial. When a black porter at the Charleston hotel that James is leaving puts down in the mud of the street the dressing case which, in the crowded bus to the railroad station, he will have to hold in his lap, he deplores "the deep seated ineptitude of the negro race for any alertness of personal service" and wonders whether it is for *this* that "the old planters, the cotton gentry, had fought and fallen." And he has not said anything truly significant about the beautiful Florida beaches and jungles when he bewails the dearth of human history attached to them. Yet even here, even at his shrillest, James has a point to make. If the sole trace of man in a landscape is in the paraphernalia of the vacation spot, if, as he puts it, the only evidence of human attachment is in what he calls the "hotel spirit," then even the most radiant beauties of nature will not dispossess that spirit of its supremacy. Look at Florida today.

What is most significant in *The American Scene* is James's sense of the spirit of contemporary America. In 1907 a European reader might shake his head and sniff: "Well, after all, what else can one expect of a nation of travelling salesmen?" But almost a century later readers everywhere may reflect: "But that's not just America. That's us, too, alas." For the modernization and commercialization and standardization and, if you will, the vulgarization of the planet merely started in America, and there only because of the richness of the land. Those things were not only American but twentieth-century phenomena. Kipling's prediction of East and West that "never the twain shall meet" was read in a cloudy crystal ball. They have met in traffic-jammed streets lined with oblong glass towers from Cádiz to Cathay.

What James most importantly saw in the new century was that it was essentially a people's thing. Make no mistake, he warns us; the "people" like the noise, the racket, the crowding, the rush, the push, the availability of gadgets, the sentimentality of entertainment, the promiscuity of human contact. For all its tycoons and robber barons and bigots and racists, the America of 1905 was still at heart a people's republic. And James at the end had no desire to be a part of it. When he went home to the blessed solitude and quiet of his beloved Lamb House, in Rye on the English Channel, it was to be for good. Actually, he was to make one more trip across the Atlantic, but only to be with his dying brother William at the end.

On an early visit to William in Chocorua in the late summer of 1905 James found himself at first enchanted by the New Hampshire countryside, where the leaves were just turning red and yellow, and by the woods and glens, which he described as "Sicilian, Theocritan, poetic, romantic, academic, from their not bearing the burden of too much history." But what was too much history? Didn't the phrase hint that he suspected already that for him at least there was too little? America had less past than Europe, and she seemed intent on destroying such precious relics of it as she still had.

Well, he could hardly blame Mother Nature for the lack of ruined castles or battle sites in the wilderness. Gazing up at the hills, he reflected that he was in the presence of a world created for "things that wouldn't, after all, happen: more the pity for them and for me and for you." It must be his function to discover "an elegance in the commonest objects and a mystery even in accidents that merely represented, perhaps, mere plainness unashamed." This would take the eye of a Cézanne.

But it was the old European tourist rather than the post-impressionist of Provence who recoiled at length against an "unagricultured" landscape, pathetically "feminine" in its gentle anxiety to please, and began to solace himself with literary metaphors. So, a solitary maple on a woodside flaming in single scarlet recalled to him "nothing so much as the daughter of a noble house dressed for a fancy ball, with the whole family gathered around to admire her before she goes."

And where history, great history, had indeed been made, as in Concord, Massachusetts, birthplace of liberty, he found, by a sleepy tranquil village, a full, slow, meadowy river which seemed to confess that it had watched the ancient fight without so much as a quickening of its current, and he could not but wonder whether one would "know for oneself what had formerly been the matter here if one hadn't happened to be able to get round behind, in the past, as it were, and more or less understand."

Later on his tour, on a visit to Washington, he was to ask the same question of Mount Vernon. The site, of course, was peerless, but the mansion was almost commonplace. Would one have thrilled in the same way had one not known it was the home of the founding father? But here he brushed aside the inquiry as inane. "The whole thing *is* Washington — not his invention and his property, but his presence and his person; with discriminations (as distinguished from enthusiasms) as invidious and unthinkable as if they were addressed to his very ears."

Only in Independence Hall, in Philadelphia, was he to find a monument worthy of the great historical event that had taken place there. He could fancy, under the high spring of the ceiling and before the great embrasured window sashes of the principal room, someone exclaiming: "What an admirable place for a Declaration of something! What could one here — what *couldn't* one really declare! I say — why not our independence?"

But before the questions raised by Mount Vernon and Philadelphia, while he was still being intrigued by the meagerness of the New England countryside, he noted that the real amusement of his trip might lie precisely in the paucity of the historical signposts. "Yes, it was actually going to be *drama*: the great adventure of a society reaching out into the apparent void for the amenities" and taking the short cut. Would the short cut be a substitute for "troublesome history, for the long, immitigable process of time"?

He would answer his query at last in the negative, but that, anyway, was to be his book. And it was, as he foresaw, to be a drama. The houses, hotels and skyscrapers, the libraries, colleges and hospitals, become anthropomorphous as characters in the story; they speak out for themselves, bragging, apologizing, threatening, cajoling and sometimes even whimpering in fear or self-pity. With their human occupants, builders and destroyers, they make up a formidable cast.

It was the New England village that gave James his first hint of a certain monotony in American manners, of the emergence of a single standard in mores and behavior. The prim white houses, the elm-shaded lanes, the chaste, unadorned temples of worship seemed the appointed sphere of the common man and woman, there being so marked an abeyance "of any wants, any tastes, any habits, any traditions but theirs." Indeed, he was actually relieved to learn that more might be going on behind the alabaster façades than met the eye, that some of the habitations could be likened to whitened sepulchres and their seemingly innocent look qualified by "a shade of the darkness of Cenci drama, of monstrous legend, of old Greek tragedy."

When the New England landscape had been let alone, it might be too bare, too plain, but that was better than when it had been despoiled. James was very stern about what the rich summer colonists had done to the idyllic Newport of his early years: that land of "a thousand delicate secret places . . . small mild points and promontories, far away little lovely sandy coves, rock set lily-sheeted ponds, almost hidden, and shallow Arcadian summer-haunted valleys." He likened this earlier Newport and its crass successor to a lovely little white hand, the back of which one might respectfully kiss, suddenly crammed with gold. And as for the summer "cottages," those ungainly white mammoths, whose owners seemed to wonder what was to be done with them, he issued the stiff answer that there was nothing to be done with them, but "to let them stand there always, vast and blank, for reminder to those concerned of the prohibited degrees of witlessness and of the peculiarly awkward vengeances of affronted proportion and discretion."

What James did not foresee was that these same "cottages" in our day would be preserved as popular museums and attract hundreds of thousands of summer visitors. But had he only applied consistently his theory that what he disliked in

America was precisely what "the crowd" wanted, he would have predicted the creation and great success of the Newport Preservation Society.

In Boston he suffered a peculiar shock at the speed of the inexorable forces of demolition. He had been as pleased as surprised to discover in a devastated Ashburton Place the survival of two little houses of which in the old days he had been particularly fond, but returning only weeks later to reconfirm this pleasant impression he was faced with a gaping hole in the ground. "Both the houses had been levelled and the space to the corner cleared; hammer and pick-axe had evidently begun to swing on the very morrow of my previous visit — which moreover had been precisely the imminent doom announced, without my understanding it, in the poor scared faces."

Wherever he went, in New York and Washington as well as in Boston, he was impressed by the transient air of even the newest and tallest structures, even of the giant skyscrapers, which made the profile of Manhattan resemble an inverted comb and which doomed their occupants to be forever "hoisted or lowered by machinery." No matter how much steel and stone went into their making, their multiple windows, like sad eyes, proclaimed their apprehension of ultimate demolition. James likened them to prisoners of the French Revolution waiting grimly for the daily roll call of the morrow's executions.

He waxed more and more critical as he toured. He came to the conclusion that the basic American formula for happiness was to "make so much money that you won't, that you don't 'mind,' don't mind anything." That for him had to be how it worked. The rich had their palaces and their motor cars; the lower sort profited "by the enormous extension of those material facilities which may be gregariously enjoyed." The latter were able "to rush about, as never under the sun before, in promiscuous packs and hustled herds." And James would not have been surprised to learn that the continued expansion of material facilities would in a couple of decades come near to guaranteeing a motor car to every American family.

The big white houses on the seashore of Deal, New Jersey, which he had seen on the first day of his trip, seemed to confirm James's conclusion. What had their message been to him but: "We don't in the least care what becomes of us after we have served our present purpose." And that purpose was simply to demonstrate the wealth of their occupants.

The two new temples that for James most exemplified the American soul were the giant hotel and the country club. In both he insisted on perceiving the essence of the democratic spirit. The gilded labyrinths of the Waldorf-Astoria were almost home and fireside to hundreds of huge-hatted ladies. "Here was a conception of publicity *as* the vital medium, organized with the authority with which the American genius for organization, put on its mettle, alone could organize it."

Was democracy then a matter of no privacy? Under that test the Versailles of Louis XIV would have been democratic. But James meant only that publicity was an element of it. The country club, with its great emphasis on the family, the bigger the better, and its stress on children — the young being, if anything, almost preferred to the old — struck him as the Eden to which any former alien, any former underdog from the farms and slums of Europe, might attain admittance once he had passed the American test of financial independence. Some of us today may see the country club as a citadel of snobbery and racial discrimination, but if one considers the standards for admission in the gentlemen's clubs of Paris and London, one can get a glimmer of what James meant.

"Family," he admitted, was, goodness knows, an important enough element in European society, but as a vertical concept stretching forward and backward in time, not, as here, as a horizontal one, expressing itself more in numbers than name.

Among the very rich, along such avenues as Fifth in New York and Bellevue in Newport, James found the signs of democracy less in evidence, and he noted particularly the rigid division of the sexes. The men were all at work "downtown"; so long as they were not interrupted in their obsessive money-making, they were quite willing that the usufruct of their labor be dispensed at will by their "uptown" wives and daughters. Social life was entirely ruled by the latter, and European aristocratic manners and ways sedulously copied. This gave to their entertainments an air of curious obsolescence, which James aptly analyzed in this passage which, if little relevant to our own day, caught the essence of his:

> The scene of our feast was a palace and the perfection of setting and service absolute; the ladies, beautiful, gracious and glittering with gems, were in tiaras and a semblance of court trains, a sort of prescribed official magnificence; but it was impossible not to ask oneself with what, in the wide American frame, such great matters might be supposed to consort or rhyme. The material pitch was so high that it carried with it really no social sequence, no application, and that, as a tribute to the ideal, to the exquisite, it wanted company, support, some sort of consecration. The difficulty, the irony of the hour was that so many of the implications of completeness, that is, of a sustaining social order, were absent. There was nothing for us to do at eleven o'clock — or for the ladies at least — but to scatter and go to bed. There was nothing, as in London or in

Paris to go "on" to; the going "on" is, for the New York aspiration, always the stumbling block. A great court-function would alone have met the strain.

In Washington, at least, James found the male less shackled to business and more in charge of the social scene. Here he found the parties delightful, albeit more populated by government functionaries than representatives of the people, though there was always a sprinkling of senators. Indeed, he dubbed the capital the "city of conversation." It seems possible that he may have regarded the very special society in which he found himself warmly welcomed, that of Henry Adams, Secretary of State John Hay and Senator Henry Cabot Lodge, as more typical of Washington than it really was.

James did not conceal his alarm at what grave changes might be wrought in the image of the essentially Anglo-Saxon Protestant America in which he had been raised by the flood tide of European immigration. He had felt in Ellis Island the "chill that comes over the native American" when he senses "the degree in which it is his American fate to share the sanctity of his American consciousness, the intimacy of his American patriotism with the inconceivable alien." And he deplored the demeaning effect of the American experience on the new arrival, how rapidly it despoiled him "of the manners which were the grace by which one had most admired him in his native habitat."

James also saw clearly enough that the steadily increasing numbers of aliens would militate against ultimate assimilation by making it easier and more acceptable for foreigners to remain foreign, and that the effect on the language could not but be marked. The accent of the future, he opined, might be "the most beautiful on the globe" (which I doubt he for a moment believed), but "we shall not know it for English." What he did not foresee was the total survival of Spanish as the accepted language, even officially, of large metropolitan districts today. But one doubts it would have much surprised him.

It would be too much to have expected James, in a year's visit, constantly travelling, to have contributed much to the understanding of our major social problems, but he was never unaware of them. He could do little more than shake his head as he gazed ruefully out his train window at the endless desolation of Southern rural areas. "It was monstrous," he wrote, to view impoverished blacks and "poor white trash" from "cushioned and kitchened Pullmans [and] to deny one's fellow creatures any claim to a personality, but that was what one was doing." And his reaction, when he ended one such journey in Biltmore, George Vanderbilt's fantastic palace high in the mountains of North Carolina, was that at last someone in the area had "cared" enough to create even that.

His only reference to what might have to be done about ameliorating the condition of the blacks was a word of caution to Northerners not to be too officious. Watching a group of "tatterdamelion darkies" lounging and sunning themselves at a railroad station was enough to convince him that, no matter how beautiful a part "sweet reasonableness" might play in the solution of racial problems, "the lips of the non-resident were, at all events, not the lips to utter this wisdom." We have seen, of course, as James could not have seen, that a hands-off policy in the rest of the nation contributed little to desegregation or black voting. But James might have drawn a hint of the real problem from the young Virginian whom he had met and liked in the Richmond museum of Civil War relics. Though he "wouldn't have hurt a Northern fly, there were things (ah, we had touched on some of these!) that, all fair, engaging, smiling, as he stood there, he would have done to a Southern negro."

And so, as so often, even if he had no remedy, James at least saw the problems.

At the end of his book he gave vent to a passionate protest at what he considered the rape of a continent so violent that he omitted it from the American edition.

> If I were one of the painted savages you have dispossessed, or even some tough reactionary trying to emulate him, what you are making would doubtless impress me more than what you are leaving unmade; for in that case it wouldn't be to *you* I should be looking in any degree for beauty or for charm. Beauty and charm would be for me in the solitude you have ravaged, and I should owe you my grudge for every disfigurement and every violence, for every wound with which you have caused the face of the land to bleed. No, since I accept your ravage, what strikes me is the long list of the arrears of your undone; and so constantly, right and left, that your pretended message of civilization is but a colossal recipe for the *creation* of arrears, and of such as can remain forever out of hand. You touch the great lonely land — and one feels it still to be — only to plant upon it some ugliness about which, never dreaming of the grace of apology or contrition, you then proceed to brag with a cynicism all your own.

But there are few on our planet today, from the ivory poachers of Africa to the wreckers of the Brazilian rain forest to the slaughterers of the whale, who can point the finger at America. Indeed, if anything, we are the leaders in the fight for conservation. James would surely have been with us.

SARAH ORNE JEWETT

⁂

LITERARY SPINSTERS in old New England are often associated with a single house, the family homestead where they continued to reside, alone or with maiden sisters, after their parents died. Emily Dickinson lived all her life in the family home in Amherst, as did Amy Lowell in Sevenels in Brookline. The white mansion that Sarah Orne Jewett's seafaring and prosperous grandfather had purchased in South Berwick, Maine, was the finest in town. Its interior was decorated with elaborate, dentilated cornices, paneled wainscoting, and arches resting on fluted columns, and it was furnished with Chippendale and Sheraton. Sarah as a child lived in the simpler neighboring abode of her father, a country doctor, but in later life, after his death and those of her grandparents, she moved into the great house and occupied it until her own death, in 1909. She was always to feel a deep nostalgia for the departed days of South Berwick's glory as a busy seaport, and never quite reconciled herself to the smoky mills that now engaged energies once devoted to the nobler calling of the sea. Her last novel, *The Tory Lover*, depicting her home town in Revolutionary days, is bathed in the sentiment of a lifetime.

Her father, however, had eschewed both sea and sea trade; he had been a beloved general practitioner, driving over the countryside in all weathers to attend births and deaths and to give what comfort and cure he could to the ailing. Years after his death, when they were elderly, his daughters were still known as the "doctor's girls." Sarah used to go with him on his rounds and seriously entertained the idea of becoming a doctor herself, but acute attacks of rheumatoid arthritis, which were to plague her all her life and finally to kill her, at the age of fifty-nine, prevented fulfillment of this youthful dream. She adopted instead the life of the cultivated young lady of the time: she rode; she sat on charitable committees; she went often to nearby Boston to visit friends, attend lectures, and in particular to hear the inspiring sermons of the great Phillips Brooks in Trinity Church.

Indeed, her deep and lasting concern with religion was to mar some of the joy she derived from her passionate reading of fiction. She didn't like, for example, the characters in Henry James's *The American*, which was serialized in *The Atlantic* when she was twenty-seven, nor did she approve of the "moral" of the tale, and she missed in George Eliot's writing "the least suggestion of our having a true and real relationship with God." Nothing, however, would keep her from admiring and reading these masters; it was simply that she resolved that a dimension missing in their work should not be missing in her own.

Jane Austen and Thackeray were her particular favorites. *Vanity Fair* was for her Tolstoy, Zola and Turgenev "all rolled in one," and *Pendennis* seemed to her greater than *Anna Karenina* and "more full of true humanity." She would be a Victorian to the end. The conquering soldier and the romantic poet were her heroes. "No two men I have ever seen came up to Grant and Tennyson in *greatness*," she would one day exclaim.

That she should have started to write early, with contributions to *The Atlantic*, was in the New England tradition. She received enthusiastic encouragement from the editor, William Dean Howells, who wisely noted her remarkable skill in reproducing the dialect of plain Maine farm folk. "You've got an uncommon feeling for *talk* — I *hear* your people," he wrote her. It is interesting that her literary career should have opened and closed with the same form: the loose-leaf novel, in which the narrator gives the reader sketches of persons and places in small Maine villages, frequently allowing one of the persons sketched to tell the narrator a longish tale of family comedy or tragedy. Jewett must have had some sense from the beginning that this was the right medium for her talent; whenever she laid it aside, as she too often did, she achieved something less memorable. It was a pity she did not have a Henry James to warn her, as he did the monologist Ruth Draper, when she asked him whether she should not, for once anyway, appear in a play with other actors: "My dear, you have woven your own little magic carpet: *stand* on it!"

It hardly matters whether a writer has a limited field if he excels in it. Only a fool would want Jane Austen to write about the Napoleonic wars or Thackeray about the slums of London. Jewett took all she needed of life from her villages and farms. As her biographer, Paula Blanchard, sees it in *Sarah Orne Jewett*, her stories express a transcendentalism "warmer and more human-scented" than Emerson's, "domesticated and particularized, based less on mystical experience than on the breathing reality of daily life." Jewett does not stint the evils that she saw among Maine country people. Insanity, suicide, loneliness, bitter poverty, wife abuse and alcoholism inhabit her pages. But these are all a bearable part of the whole. Most of her people, most of the time, can still cope. And wild creatures and plants, as Blanchard observes, are both embodiments and messengers of universal anima: "Birds in particular serve as a kind of ironic commentary on the limited perceptions of human beings. During the walking funeral [the procession from church to graveyard] the song sparrows 'sang and sang, as if with previous knowledge of immortality, and contempt for those who could so pettily concern themselves with death.' "

The Library of America has wisely concentrated its edition of Jewett on these Maine stories. Of course, all are not equally well conceived. The difference between success and failure in Jewett's delicate art was always a hairline. The danger that stalked her was sentimentality.

Interestingly enough, Flaubert, the least sentimental of novelists, was one of her literary models, and she kept two maxims gleaned from his work pinned before her when she was writing: "Write about daily life as you would write history," and "It is not to provoke laughter, nor tears nor rage, but to act as nature does, that is, to provoke dreaming." Yet however painstaking she was in selecting the *mot juste* for her fine descriptions of Maine landscapes and seascapes, Jewett totally eschewed Flaubert's emotional disengagement from his characters, believing firmly that her talent had been given her by God for the moral improvement of her readers. I think Blanchard makes the best possible case for this attitude. "Stated that way," she writes, "[Jewett's] faith might seem to resemble the most banal and sentimental of Victorian platitudes, an embroidered plaque hung on the wall. But because she was who she was, it simply confirmed the strength she already possessed, fostering her native capacities for sympathy and language and freeing her to express them fully through friendship and work."

Having dealt with Jewett's relationship with God, we may now proceed, in the approved fashion of our day, to her relationship with her fellow mortals. She never married. Was she a lesbian? John Greeleaf Whittier asked her once, "Sarah, was thee ever in love?" to which her startled reply was "No! Whatever made you think of that?" Of course, she meant she had never been in love with a *man*. But what about Annie Fields, the brilliant widow of her famed publisher, James T. Fields, in whose Boston house on Charles Street Jewett lived for months at a time in the last half of her life and with whom she travelled all over Europe, meeting the celebrities of the literary and political worlds? I think most readers today would go along with Blanchard's conclusion that this was what was known as a "Boston marriage," a semi-homoerotic friendship, entirely approved of in its day, without any physical sexual expression. But I think Blanchard underestimates us when she says that such a relationship is "hardly imaginable to the modern sensibility."

Deephaven, Jewett's first book, was published in 1877, when she was twenty-eight. It provides a beautiful but uneven start to the long series of Maine short stories that was to reach perfection twenty years later in her masterpiece, *The Country of the Pointed Firs*. Two young city girls go to spend the summer in a Maine coastal village that has just been inherited by the family of one of them. Their enthusiasm is infectious but superficial; the little book is more like a graceful vacation letter than a novel. It was followed by three small collections of stories and essays: *Old Friends and New*, *Country By-Ways* and *The Mate of the Daylight*, which all have charm, if a slightly pale and wistful one. And then in 1884 Jewett tried her hand at a more conventional form of novel.

A Country Doctor is drawn in part from Jewett's memories of her father's visits to the sick, on which she often accompanied him. The heroine, Anna, like her creator, wants to become a doctor; but unlike Jewett she succeeds in her goal, giving up, almost cheerfully, all idea of marriage, even though she has an ardent and eligible swain. There is an amusing scene when, at a picnic, Anna rudely dispels her beau's Victorian ideas about the weaker sex by yanking, with one quick practiced pull, the dislocated arm bone of a farmer back into its socket. But the lectures that Jewett inserts, as a frank propagandist, on the role of women in the professions are, of course, of little present interest and interrupt the flow of the narrative.

Dr. Jewett's death, in 1878, was a sad blow to Sarah and intensified her reluctance to take her place in a world of adults. Annie Fields, who to some extent took her father's place in her mind and heart, pointed out that her friend was a curious combination of the immature and the advanced. "She never put her dolls away and always used her child-names, but her plans were large and sometimes startling to others." Three years after her father's death Jewett was writing about him with the same kind of loving whimsicality that one finds in the letters of Emily Dickinson. "Today is Father's birthday. I wonder if people keep the day they die for another birthday after they get to heaven? I have been thinking of him a great deal this last day or two. I wonder if I am doing all the things he wishes I would do, and I hope he does not get tired of me."

With *The Country of the Pointed Firs* in 1896, near the end of her writing life, Jewett returned to the fine straight highway of her first book, but now with all the experience of twenty rich years of observing and recording. The narrator of the novel, never named but a lady writer of middle years, comes to spend the summer in the coastal village of Dunnet, where she boards with Almira Todd, a widowed herb grower who supplements the work of the local doctor. For fifty cents a week the narrator rents the empty schoolhouse in which to do her writing, but her attention and soon her heart are quickly absorbed by the villagers. Mrs. Todd takes her about to meet everybody and fills in any missing background with stories. Captain Littlepage, cozily crazy, gives her an eerie account of the wraith-like creatures who inhabit the North Pole. She visits Shell-heap Island, where "poor Joanna Todd," crossed in love, has died a recluse, and hears her story; she attends the great reunion of the Bowden clan, a huge family picnic that includes everyone, for nearly everyone is kin. This is the special ceremony of the summer, a kind of fertility rite. She goes out to Green Island to meet Mrs. Todd's wonderfully spry octogenarian mother, Mrs. Blackett, adored by the neighborhood, and her bachelor brother, whose forty-year courtship of Esther Hight, the mature Dunnet "shepherdess," culminates in marriage and makes a fit ending for the book. And finally she meets Mrs. Martin, the "Queen's twin," who was born on the same day as Queen Victoria and who has given her children the names of the princes and princesses. Her little cottage is filled with newspaper and magazine pictures of the glorious reign. The whole portrait of Dunnet is filled with emotion, but very little of it can be expressed. A New England reserve covers all. When our guide takes her leave of Mrs. Todd in the end, she cannot quite bear it, feeling that some demonstration is at last called for, but she is firmly checked: "I could not part so; I ran after her to say good-by, but she shook her head and waved her hand without looking back when she heard my hurrying steps, and so went away down the street."

To me the most beautiful of all Jewett's tales is "A White Heron." Sylvia, a little girl who lives in a hut in the woods with her grandmother, Mrs. Tilley, is guiding their one old cow home from grazing when she encounters a handsome young ornithologist who shoots birds to mount and study them. He is intensely eager to obtain a rare white heron that has been sighted in the neighborhood. He will pay ten dollars for information about it, a fortune for the Tilleys. Sylvia has seen the lovely bird, but does not tell him. She takes the young man to her grandmother, who puts him up for a couple of nights. The three become very friendly; Sylvia now makes a romantic hero of him. But on the second night she steals out of the house in early dawn and, at the risk of her life, climbs a gigantic pine, on top of which she finds the heron's nest. When she returns, the old grandmother and the hunter, rightly suspecting where she has been, beg her to tell them what she has seen. But she cannot. "The murmur of the pine's green branches is in her ears; she remembers how the white heron came flying through the golden air and how they watched the sea and the morning together, and Sylvia cannot speak; she cannot tell the heron's secret and give its life away."

Of course, there have been modern critics who see in the great pine that Sylvia so painfully climbs a phallic symbol. I don't think Jewett would have cared for that theory, and although it interested and amused me for a while, I at length rejected it. If the tree, like the young man's gun, is a symbol of male force and destructiveness, it also provides shelter and safety for the heron's young.

Blanchard attributes the neglect of Jewett's work in the fifteen years between her death and Willa Cather's re-arousal of interest in it to the patronizing tone of "male literary pundits." Indeed, she regards this tone as a "classic illustration of historic male bias in the canon." I don't agree. It seems to me that fiction is one of the rare fields in which women have shared equal honors with men, and the ultimate judges, *i.e.*, the readers, have had a majority of women. I believe what Jewett suffered from, and will always suffer from, is the kind of reader, of either sex, who cannot be convinced that her subject material is important. There are people who still say that about Jane Austen; Henry James even said it about Flaubert, and Theodore Roosevelt said it about Henry James. Anatole France said it about Proust, Edith Wharton about Joyce . . . there is no end to that sort of criticism. And some persons are never going to believe that two semiliterate old farmers' widows sitting on a crumbling back porch in a decayed Maine coastal village are going to have much to say that will interest them. Even the fine Library of America edition of Jewett is not going to make *them* change their minds.

ROBERT GRANT

※ ※ ※

R OBERT GRANT (1852–1940), for thirty years a judge of the Probate Court of Suffolk County in Massachusetts and the author of many popular novels of manners, led one of those long sunny lives of prominent Bostonians of his era, full of friends and honors and benevolent chuckles, with a loving happy family and many congenial clubs, such interesting public responsibilities as being a Harvard overseer and alumni president, and with ties by blood and friendship to all the first families in town. And what is more, none of it was wasted on him. He thoroughly enjoyed it all. His *vers de société* were in demand at every anniversary or commemorative event, and his memoirs, published when he was eighty-three, are the amiable account of decades of pleasure and duty intertwined.

It may be that readers of *Fourscore* today, if any there be, will find that the author places too great an emphasis on ancestry — he is fatiguing about the Scottish Highland origins of the Grants — or that he finds more delights in Boston social life than a less "clubbable" man might, nor is it easy to go along with his preference for women as angels of the home or his manifest distrust of any change in social manners or mores, but few would dispute that he was a man of wit and kindliness and of the highest moral principles.

But 1927 marked a watershed in his life. In that year Governor Alvin T. Fuller created an advisory committee to counsel him on the question of commuting the death sentences of Nicola Sacco and Bartolomeo Vanzetti for the murders in 1920 of a paymaster and his assistant in South Braintree. To this committee he appointed A. Lawrence Lowell, president of Harvard, Samuel W. Stratton, president of the Massachusetts Institute of Technology, and Judge Grant. The panel examined the judicial record and found no critical errors; they concluded that justice had been done. The defendants were executed.

In the torrent of indignation that swept America and Europe, the advisory board was pilloried. Grant was accused of every conceivable tory prejudice and immortalized in Ben Shahn's devastating mural *The Passion of Sacco and Vanzetti*, where he is depicted, grim-faced, holding a lily over the open caskets of the dead men. It was even averred that he had hated Italians ever since his luggage was stolen in a railway station in Venice.

The defense that he offered for the committee in his memoirs was brief and dignified:

> We were accused . . . with being compliant tools of a capitalist conspiracy, with an excessive reverence for the courts of the Commonwealth, with a lack of moral and intellectual sympathy that blinded us to essential justice . . . all [of us] had been schooled to hold the balance even between the powerful and the lowly, the rich and the poor, as the first principle of humane authority. Is it conceivable that we men, belonging to a conscientious

generation, should have been so spiritually impervious to justice as to be willing to reject the plea of two foreigners of humble birth . . . ?

But to G. Louis Joughin and Edmund M. Morgan, authors of *The Legacy of Sacco and Vanzetti*, Grant was unfitted by his character and background to give a fair judgment in the case. Theirs is the kind of argument we have recently seen reduced to absurdity in the O. J. Simpson case. It is virtually impossible to find a judge or juror without *some* flaw of prejudice. The authors concede, a bit condescendingly, that Grant was "a man of modest wealth, traveled, well read, the author of numerous pleasantly innocuous novels," but insist that he had "almost no consciousness of the economic and social problems faced by the industrial society in which he lived." Even assuming that to be true, which it manifestly was not, about a man who in addition to his experience as a trial judge had been a state commissioner and secretary to a governor, does one need to be an expert on economic and social problems to determine whether or not a murder has been committed?

No, the authors' real thrust against Grant is contained in another indictment. *Instead* of the social consciousness that should have been evidenced in *Fourscore*

we have a photograph of a youthful costume party; those in the group are A. Lawrence Lowell, Katherine Parkman (Mrs. J. T. Coolidge), Harriet Lawrence (Mrs. Augustus Hemenway), Harcourt Amory, Anna Lowell (Mrs. A. Lawrence Lowell), Katherine Lowell (Mrs. James Roosevelt), Percival Lowell, Francis C. Lowell, Flora Grant (Mrs. Morris Gray), and the author. The picture is a splendid obverse of a New England medal, the other side of which would show Vanzetti's dozen Italian alibi witnesses.

The difference between those who find the inclusion of such a photograph in a book of memoirs a disqualification to judge a crime, and those, like myself, who deem it an irrelevance, is unbridgeable. At any rate there has been a considerable revision of opinion on the issues in the Sacco-Vanzetti case, and many probers now believe that Sacco at least was guilty.

Of Grant's fiction only *Unleavened Bread* (1900) and *The Chippendales* (1909) are remembered today. The former created something of a sensation when it appeared and is quite unlike any of his other books. The heroine, or at least the protagonist, Selma White, at first appears to Wilbur Lyttleton, the hero or quasi-hero, as he, and perhaps Grant as well, liked to visualize a future bride: "a white-souled angel of light clad in the graceful outlines of flesh, an Amazon, and yet a winsome, tender spirit, and above all a being imbued with the stimulating intellectual independence he had been taught to associate with American womanhood." Selma herself, however, is as far as possible from this description.

Grant wrote later that he had once awakened in the middle of the night and "suddenly, without much exercise of will, Selma White's entire career evolved from my imagination, with all the attendant characters and most of the episodes." Certainly her character aroused so many cries of recognition among readers that she had to have been a definite and well-known American type. Edith Wharton wrote Grant that she was "as good in her way as Gwendolyn Grandcourt," George Eliot's gold-digger in *Daniel Deronda*.

Bliss Perry assured him that no one would ever have to do his book over again, that he had fixed the type as irrevocably as Flaubert did in *Madame Bovary*. And Theodore Roosevelt was of the opinion that if Grant's was "a melancholy, indeed a painful book," it was still "the strongest study of American life that has been written for many years."

Yet what is Selma? I doubt that her counterpart exists today. She is Middle Western, the daughter of a country physician, who has grown up during the Civil War and made a loveless marriage to a dull but rising dealer in varnish in order to be able to move to the bustling small town of Benham and share in its bustling future. She is imbued with a strong faith in her native land: "To be an American meant to be more keenly alive to the responsibility of life than any other citizen of civilization, and to be an American woman meant to be something finer, cleverer, stronger and purer than any other daughter of Eve." And the heroic deeds of the Civil War have served in her early years to intensify this faith.

Yet this patriotism is a religion devoid of ethics, education or even taste. Selma converts her belief that all men are equal to a conviction that nobody can be superior in any way to Selma and that Selma must therefore rule the roost. Finding her husband to be a social hindrance as she climbs above him, she divorces him for a casual adultery, the result of her refusal to co-habit. She then marries a New York architect, whom she drives to an early death from overwork and worry in trying to make the fortune needed for the social position that she now recognizes will not be accorded to her merit alone. She returns to Benham, where she at last attains the success that she feels to be her due by marrying a dishonest politician who becomes both rich and a senator by ratting on his dishonest backers.

Selma is consistently odious. She cares for none of her husbands, nor for her only child, who dies. She uses her social and political power to staff the hospital, whose board she dominates, with quacks who flatter her prejudices and seeks to destroy any who dare to oppose her. The only halfway decent thing she does in the whole book is to refuse alimony from her first husband, even though she is penniless and must work to support herself. I confess I do not understand this refusal — it certainly separates her from the other mercenary beauties of literature. Yet Grant seems to find in it an essential trait of her peculiar brand of Americanism.

Well, there she stands, anyway, the central figure of this strangely interesting novel, certainly the author's most significant contribution to American letters. Sinclair Lewis and Theodore Dreiser, I am sure, would have recognized her. What strikes me as most singular about her is her laziness: she feels herself so *entitled* to everything that she won't even stoop to dirty tricks until she finds that everything has not been poured into her lap. As her ex-friend Flossie Williams tells her:

> You're one of those American women — I've always been curious to meet one in all her glory — who believe they are born in the complete panoply of flawless womanhood; that they are by birthright consummate housewives, leaders of the world's thought and ethics, and peerless society queens. All this by instinct, by heritage and without education. That's what you believe, isn't it? And now you are offended because you haven't been invited to become a leader of New York society. You don't understand, and I don't suppose you ever will understand, that a true lady — a genuine society queen — represents modesty and sweetness and self-control, and gentle thoughts and feelings; that she is evolved by gradual thoughts and processes from generation to generation, not ready made.

Perhaps Grant gives away one of his prejudices here. He has a weakness for "genuine" society queens. But while it is perfectly true that such must demonstrate some degree of charm or attractiveness, it is often only the appearance of these qualities that is needed. Flossie should have warned Selma to develop at least a minimum of allure. Grant made the same mistake with Selma that Edith Wharton (whom he immensely admired and personally liked) had made with Undine Spragg, in *The Custom of the Country*; both characters are too obviously unlovable to have caught the men they are depicted as catching. Both indeed are endowed with physical beauty — their authors, evidently, aware of the problem, keep insisting on that — but beauty is not enough for a sexually cold and unimaginative woman — at least for any but a very young and very naïve first husband. The trouble was that Wharton and Grant *disliked* their heroines too much. Thackeray had a sneaking fondness for Becky Sharp, and even the stern George Eliot had a certain tolerance for the frivolous Gwendolyn.

Grant's second surviving novel, *The Chippendales*, is the long but fairly lively tale of two vividly contrasted young Bostonian males, Hugh Blaisdell, the slick, fast-talking *arriviste*, who makes the biggest fortune in town and marries into the oldest family, and Henry Sumner, an idealistic puritan and a distaff member of that same family, who forfeits a fortune rather than meet the condition stipulated in the will of a maternal aunt that he change his name to Chippendale. Grant tries to be fair to both his protagonists; he endows Blaisdell with generosity and public spirit while condemning his gulling the public for personal gain, and he demonstrates the occasional absurdity of Sumner's strict but scrupulous conscientiousness. He sees, in short, that such a metropolis as Boston cannot stand still and that changes are not *all* for the bad . . . though he wonders a bit about this.

The book is certainly a perceptive and amusing picture of Boston society at the turn of the century by an insider who knew "everyone," and will continue to be read, like J. P. Marquand's *The Late George Apley*, as much for its sociological as for its literary value. But there are moments when the author's anti-feminism and nostalgia for the "good old days" prove trying. I suppose there is always a question of how much one should let oneself be put off by an artist's prejudice. Should it matter that Wagner obviously considered Alberich and Mime as prototypes of Jews or that Shakespeare libelled Joan of Arc in *Henry VI*? Grant does not put his readers to quite such tests, but we stir uneasily at Sumner's wedding to Priscilla Avery, in the happy ending of the novel, when the groom's mother, watching her beloved son at the altar, "solved the rapt expression" on his face with the Miltonic phrase "He for God only, she for God in him."

And the "sweetness" of the bride's surrender "still lingered in Priscilla's brow and her loveliness wore the glorified charms of the bride who has no doubts."

Thackeray, one must admit, for all his irony, would have been quite capable of such a sentence: one has only to go back to Laura Pendennis. But Thackeray, in what Robert Grant considered the greatest novel ever written, was also the creator of Becky Sharp.

THE ABBÉ MUGNIER

❧   ❧   ❧

T HE PARIS JOURNAL of the Abbé Mugnier, which he
kept for sixty years (1879–1939), was published by Mer-
cure de France in 1985 and has unfortunately not been trans-
lated or published over here. It is the remarkable record of a
priest who knew and confessed the cream of the old aristoc-
racy of the Faubourg Saint Germain and who was also the
friend and sometimes the intimate of many of the leading literary and artistic lights of the time.

The Abbé's nobler qualities have been somewhat swamped
by his reputation as the spiritual guide of the *gratin* and by
his long-remembered quips, as, for example, his reply to the
aging actress who asked him if it was a sin for her to admire
her own beauty when she looked in a mirror: "No, my dear,
it's only an error." Or to the avid social climber who, finding
that each new level he attained was not the "true" faubourg,
asked impatiently whether the true faubourg was simply
where he *wasn't*: "I didn't want to be the one to tell you."

It is perfectly true, as the Abbé admitted in his journal, that
he loved the "great world," with its "titles, beautiful houses,
gilded panels, chandeliers, wits and celebrities," but he hoped,
as with Proust, whose good friend he became, that its attraction was largely in the romantic historical associations that it

provided for his intensely active imagination. He certainly never allowed himself to overlook the shabby aspects of society.

"These people have a way of translating their bad habits into principles," he wrote. "Emptiness and ennui are sublimated into sacred etiquette . . . No aristocrat is apt to have a true and original talent for writing. He is too *comme il faut.* There are too many servants between him and reality. Noblemen don't fraternize. Talent *tutoie.*"

And he disapproved heartily of the lady who boasted to him, in the First World War, that she had actually shaken hands with one of her footmen, who had gained the *croix de guerre.* "But you wouldn't have asked him to sit down at the dining room table with you!" one of the company who heard her exclaimed. For these people the preservation of social distinctions was as vital as winning the war.

Arthur Mugnier was born in 1853 in Lubersac, where his father had supervised the restoration of the chateau, and after the latter's early death, leaving the family with slender resources, his devout mother took him to Paris and used all of her strong influence to induce him to take holy orders. He was then a timid and naïf youth, very spiritual and fearful of sinning. With a different mother he might never have entered the church. But she was motivated, not only by her desire to create peace of mind for her son, but by her notion that she was propelling him into a career where the social ladder would be more easily scaled. In this she was more successful than she could have dreamed. When she died, in 1903, her son noted: "The poor young woman from Lorraine who came to Paris with so few prospects had dukes and princes at her obsequies!"

For it did not take a sophisticated society long to find out that there was a vicar in the neighborhood who understood the temptations of life and did not fulminate boringly about human lapses. To Mugnier, souls were souls, and it was his job to save them and not to shake his head and thunder comminations. The tolerance and wisdom that he rapidly developed, once he was free of what he had considered the mind-stifling seminary, together with his ready wit and large heart, made him as welcome in the drawing room as in the confessional. Hostesses would instruct their servants to clean or repair his worn hat and gloves and umbrella when they were left in the coat room, for he never seemed to give a thought to his appearance. Of course, some people laughed at this. The poet Anna de Noailles suggested there was an element of coquetry in his shabbiness. She may have been right.

His relations with the church and its hierarchy were never easy. He was always critical of the organizational side of the clerical establishment. In this entry of 1905 he penned a protest in the form of an imagined address to his superiors.

> You talk only of parishional and cultural associations. You spend all your energy on these. The inward faith is relegated to the bottom of the pile. And what of justice, charity, resignation, courage and all that makes up the human soul? The question of *church* kills the question of religion. Religion is a movement of the spirit, of the heart. You have made it a power, a society, an exterior force, something in conflict with other powers and other societies. In order to love God and one's neighbor, is so much materialism necessary? How far we are from what Christ wished! He wouldn't even tolerate the Temple.

And when Armageddon came in 1914, he noted that in all the years of his priesthood he had never once heard what should have been the great voice of the church denouncing hate: hate of the Republic, hate of the Jews, hate of Dreyfus, hate of Germans. The world had gone mad.

"I can only retreat into my shell . . . We should make peace, and nobody wants to. They'd rather kill a generation of Frenchmen for the sake of France. We slaughter in the name of God!"

For the first half of his ecclesiastical career the Abbé was vicar (assistant to the curé) in the Church of Saint Clotilde in the Faubourg Saint Germain, but in 1909 his friendship and hospitality to a renegade priest who had taken a wife caused such a scandal that he was advised by his superiors to resign his vicarship and go into temporary retirement. A year later he was assigned to the lower office of almoner to the Convent of the Sisters of Saint Joseph of Cluny, at an inconvenient but not unmanageable distance from his dinner parties in the old faubourg, which post he held until his final retirement. No doubt his powerful friends saved him from a more rigorous disciplining.

Fortunately, he was devoid of clerical ambitions. In 1900, nine years before his trouble with the church, he had written:

Suppose I be made a bishop, and they send me to Saint-Florin or Limoges. After the initial excitement of my jeweled mitre and my coronation I find myself buried alive in a small backwater with no society to speak of. Priests would be my daily companions, the same sort with whom I have had almost no converse since the dreary days of the seminary!

But if he had no wish for ecclesiastical preferment, he may have been tempted to sell his soul to become a great writer. Literature was the love of his life, making up for a wife and family, making up, indeed, for everything, and, wistfully acknowledging his own lack of creative talent, he resigned himself to the lesser joys of reading and the cultivation of the authors whom he admired.

His first close friend among the latter was J.-K. Huysmans, the naturalist writer, a friend and follower of Zola, and author of the exquisitely decadent novel *À Rebours*, whose protagonist was modeled on the flamboyant epicurean Robert de Montesquieu. Huysmans was endowed with a feverish imagination and a scholastic fascination with the occult. He loved to explore the dark world of satanic cults and black masses, though at the same time he was flayed by a puritanical conscience that made him gag at his own sexual proclivities. It was the Abbé who led him gently into the arms of the church and made of him a reformed and chaste penitent.

The conversion started with Huysmans's temporary retreat in 1892 into a monastery.

Last night Huysmans, on his balcony, gave his impressions, between two glasses of beer, of his visit to La Trappe. He was much troubled by obscene fantasies. He took communion twice, but the pressures and urges of the devil were such that he even contemplated suicide. The father who confessed him didn't seem surprised by this, and one monk frankly admitted to him that it was a common experience of inmates to be obsessed with sexual visions and temptations. Huysmans's retort was: "So one has no peace, even here!" Zola's only comment to him on his monastic visit was that he must be cracked.

The Abbé gained considerable fame for bringing this gifted heretic into the Roman fold, with writers as well as with the faithful. He was now sought not only as a preacher but as a lecturer on literary matters. Huysmans introduced him to his fellow authors, who, however initially suspicious of a priest at their gatherings, soon learned to welcome this gentle and charming enthusiast, who appreciated their work, enjoyed their dirty jokes without raising an eyebrow and never sought to convert them. As Bernard Berenson was later to say to the Abbé, "You are the most unprejudiced man I've ever met." Bohemia as well as the old faubourg could appreciate a perfect guest.

They would have been even more amused had they known that the Abbé was taking it all down.

November 20, 1896. Huysmans talked of the porcine pleasures of Guy de Maupassant. One evening at a party of fourteen men (Huysmans was one of them) Maupassant boasted that he could tire a woman out making love. The party then adjourned to a bordello, where Maupassant, put to the test, stripped before all and came five times with his chosen partner. Flaubert, ecstatic, cried, "How refreshing!" Huysmans asserts that there is no one more shameless than Maupassant. Another time, after he and Huysmans and Paul Bourget had dined together, and Bourget having suggested they make a night of it, they had gone to a bordello. Maupassant in the parlor where they met the girls suddenly yanked down Bourget's pants and cried out, "Is *this* all you have to show these ladies?" Bourget fled.

Decades later, in 1935, on a visit to Chartres, the Abbé, thinking back on the now long dead Huysmans and on the beautiful novel he had written about its cathedral, moaned at the intransigence of clerics who had never been touched by the sublime architecture before their eyes.

It disgusted me to recall, when Huysmans published *La Cathédrale*, the blindness of the clergy of the region. Of all the priests, curés, canons, seminary professors and bishops of the diocese of Chartres who had lived in the shadow of this magnificent monument, not one had consecrated a lasting page to its glorification. We had to wait until the end of the nineteenth century for a disciple of Zola, emerging from the sewers of naturalism, to discover, towering over the harvest fields of La Bauce, "the blonde with the blue eyes." Oh, ecclesiastical sterility!

A good half of the journal is devoted to portraits of the writers the Abbé knew. We see Anatole France "with the specious air of an old count of the Faubourg Saint Germain or perhaps rather that of a retired army officer." We hear Cocteau likening a play of Henri Bernstein's, which sought to take crude advantage of the patriotic war fever of 1917, to "a street walker in widow's weeds." And here is the poet Anna de Noailles:

She would like to be the cross, the Arc de Triomphe, Napoleon. She is the hypertrophe of myself. She knows no bounds. She should have lived in Alexandria, in Byzantium. She is the end of a race. She wants to be loved by every man who's in love with another woman. She should have mated with the sun, the wind, an element.

His first meeting with Proust was in 1917.

Marcel Proust is very distinguished-looking. He quoted a line of Oscar Wilde: "The great event of my life was the death in Balzac of Lucien de Rubempré." He told me that he was still writing books, but he didn't seem to believe that anyone read them. He spoke of cathedrals, Chartres and Reims. Reims has now the look of a woman in whose face vitriol has been flung. The Germans did this to her, according to him, out of jealousy; they have nothing like Reims in their own country. The angels of Reims have Da Vinci smiles. Proust spends most of his time in bed. He quoted the Comte Greffulhe, asking him to sign the guest book: "Just your signature, please. No comments."

The Abbé recorded later that Madame de Noailles was shocked when Proust, in the very room where his deceased mother was laid out, had offered her graceful compliments on her last book of verse. Also, that Madame de Polignac was less than complimented when Proust had offered to dedicate one of the novels of *À La Recherche* to her late husband. It was *Sodome et Gomorrhe*.

Mugnier never met Oscar Wilde, but he collected some of the sayings of Wilde's last forlorn years in Paris from those who had.

Wilde suggested that the prodigal son had abominable parents. They butchered a veal for him, knowing he hated veal. And that when the woman taken in adultery was released from her accusers, her husband turned up to cast the first stone. Judas bargained the priests up from ten to thirty pieces of silver, only to discover later that the coins were false.

Paul Valéry, like Wilde, had some novel readings of the New Testament.

May 25, 1922. Valéry confided in me that he was not a Christian and that he does not care for the New Testament, which he finds meretricious. He cannot understand the mixture of God and suffering, and he considers the miracles unworthy of a deity. The changing of water into wine was a vulgar trick of prestidigitation. And when Jesus felt the virtue run out of him when someone touched him, he did not realize that he was suffering from hemorrhoids. Nor has Valéry any use for the swine charging into the lake. He maintains that there are several different Christs in the Gospels. He defines faith as the power to fabricate the true, a matter of intellectual volition. The real duty is to doubt.

Here is a glimpse of Colette in 1922:

Dined at the Girods with Segonzac, Colette, Paul Morand, Marie Laurencin. Colette, bare-armed in a red print dress, examined all the objects in the room, touched this and that, fingered the ladies' necklaces with admiration and showed joy at everything. She talked like a child, a *gamine*, who hates restraint and discipline. She claimed she wasn't born to be a writer, that she was made to do nothing, to ride horseback, to swim, to bask in the sun. She loves to give one recipes with picturesque details: "A bouillon shouldn't be too personal."

And here is Valéry again, now in 1925:

I ran into Paul Valéry on the Boulevard Saint Germain. He talked of carnal love. Voluptuousness, the flesh, he claims, does not really exist. Carnal love is more truly con-nected with the intellect — and with the deepest part of the intellect. This is one of the curiosities of man. Sex he compares to a truffle which the desert fathers and founders

of the church turned into a kind of state affair. By invent-
ing the concept of chastity they made a mountain out of a
molehill.

This entry in 1933 juxtaposed amusingly the extremes of
the two worlds in which the Abbé lived.

Lunched yesterday with the Descoves. Céline and his
mother. The painter Vlaminck. The conversation at table
exploded like fireworks. Céline talks fast and noisily; he's a
gamin type; one senses the masses. He mimes people well,
with all necessary repetitions and *"heins."* His language was
very coarse; my priestly ears were not spared. He has been
to Berlin and says the people are close to anarchy. They
can't possibly make war now; they're too afraid of the
communists. He gave us a frightful picture of the coal town
Breslau — the Middle Ages revived. Vlaminck asked him if
he was going to continue to write about the subjects he
had been treating, and he assured us that he would — with
all their horrors. That anything else would be a desertion.
Vlaminck, for his part, roundly declared that there were no
more painters, either in France, Spain, Germany or Italy.
"*I* am a painter," he naïvely added. "If I weren't convinced
of that, I shouldn't paint. I go to a museum as to a bordello, to amuse myself, but I don't go upstairs. I don't sleep
with Delacroix and the others."
    I went home afterwards and met the queen of Portugal
at my doorstep, who had been waiting for me. She helped
me upstairs and we had a long chat.

But the writer whose work the Abbé preferred to that of
all others, whom he would have most loved to know and
to whose chateau in Brittany he made reverent periodic

pilgrimages, was François-René, Vicomte de Chateaubriand. When Mugnier died, his old servant was heard to murmur: "Oh, how happy Monsieur l'Abbé will be now! He is going to meet Monsieur le Vicomte at last." Here he is in 1917, writing at his most fulsome:

> With Chateaubriand it is love in all its forms: acuteness, voluptuousness, intensity, insatiability, pride, jealousy, desire — a gulf, a whirlpool, love devouring and devoured. The Song of Songs of passion, whose final stanza is death foreseen, sought, the death of all that limits love, the death of God, the end of the world. Love in the conflagration of Valhalla. Love as the summit, the nadir, the anarchy which destroys the object of love, which destroys all existence. Has anything ever been more radical, more logical, more mad in the order of sentiments?

As a priest the Abbé was always compassionate, certainly to a fault, in the eyes of his fellow clerics. Once, after hearing a peculiarly horrid confession, he left the booth and hurried after the departing sinner to embrace him and exclaim: "Pardoning is not enough — we must love!" He had to believe in hell, he told his parishioners — it was dogma — but he didn't have to believe there was anyone in it. Those who liked to imagine the infernal region as filled with the damned conceived of a god in their own image.

He sighed rather than blustered over the sins that were confessed to him.

"A woman can be young, beautiful, a countess and even pious and still be twice aborted of her husband's doing without telling him."

And another lovely lady wafted the tale of her adultery to

him through the grill of the confessional "in a zephyr of sweet perfume."

"Oh, the void of my life!" he exclaimed. "It is in vain that I burden myself with pious tasks or that I rush through the Faubourg Saint Germain from salon to salon. It all leaves me with a soul that is ravaged, uncertain, dead."

In 1911, after a somber visit to his oculist, he recorded a desperate prayer: "O Lord, let me not be blind! That's the only thing I ask."

The prayer was partially granted. His eyes remained more or less serviceable until 1932, when he recorded, "My life was reading. I am dead."

He survived until 1944, dying in Paris, still lucid, at the age of ninety-one. We do not have his reflections on the German occupation, as he discontinued the diary in 1939, shortly after the outbreak of war. One of the last entries records his meeting with the Duke and Duchess of Windsor.

"My eyes did not permit me to make out the features of this more or less royal couple, but I felt their cordiality. It may have been an illusion, but I had a sense of sympathy, particularly from the duchess. Apparently she asked Princess Bibesco, as she was leaving, 'Do you think the Abbé would care to dine with us one night?' "

The duke had asked him whether he remembered the terrible events in Paris of 1871. Of course he did. From the Commune to Mrs. Simpson — what a stretch of time!

F. MARION CRAWFORD

꙱   ꙱   ꙱

F RANCIS MARION CRAWFORD (1854–1909) is reputed to
have been the first American novelist to become a millionaire out of his trade. It is perhaps significant that his
background contained an unusual mixture of Yankee patriotism and European sophistication. His father, Thomas Crawford, sculpted the Indian on the dome of the Capitol in
Washington and the equestrian statue of George Washington
in Richmond, and his aunt Julia Ward Howe wrote the words
of "The Battle Hymn of the Republic," but he himself, except
for three years at Saint Paul's School in Concord, New
Hampshire, was raised in Rome amid the cultivated expatriate society of artists and writers, who lived so much better
under the favorable exchange rate of that day than they
would have at home.

Crawford's mother, born Louisa Ward of the New York
banking family, married the painter Luther Terry after her
first husband's early death, and they lived on the *piano nobile*
of the Palazzo Odescalchi, designed by Bernini. One of his
sisters married a Prussian officer, another, an English diplomat. Marion himself took the fullest advantage of his polyglot
environment; he became multilingual, as much at ease in

German, French and Italian as in his native tongue. He even studied Sanskrit. As his half-sister, Margaret Terry Chanler, described him, he was "a darling of the gods, exceedingly handsome, tall, well-built, with blazing blue eyes and very regular features, an excellent brain and universal facility."

But what was this god-favored cynosure going to do with his talents? At twenty-one he disappeared into India, where, in Allahabad, for two years he edited a newspaper. After that he went to America to consult his remarkable uncle Sam Ward, the famed bon viveur and friend of the great, a maker and loser of fortunes, known in Washington as "King of the Lobby," and his equally remarkable aunt Julia Ward Howe. Both were enthusiastically interested in the young man and determined that he should not waste himself. Should he cultivate his fine voice and become an opera singer? Or go into politics, as he seemed to prefer? Or business? Even law?

Marion assessed his own capacities with sober reflection. In a letter to his uncle he wrote:

> I believe that with merely an average intellect I possess certain peculiarities in a unique degree. I am, I believe, perfectly incapable of anything like enthusiasm, and I have not the slightest imagination. I am conscious also of the power to work my mind with absolute certainty of what it can do, at every minute of my existence. If I were to describe myself in one word, I would say "unchangeable" — slow to form an opinion and slower still to change one, slowest of all to let people know what I think.

At last Uncle Sam had a brilliant idea. Marion had told him an intriguing story about a snake charmer in India. He should write a novel about it! Aunt Julia, with whom he was staying, practically locked him in his room until he had started it, and the finished text, *Mr. Isaacs*, became an immediate best seller both in America and England, as would be most of its innumerable successors. Marion Crawford had become a household word and would remain one until his death. What he had written to his uncle about his lack of imagination was the purest poppycock, but what he had said about his own power over his mind was entirely valid. He was determined to retain the success he had achieved so young, and he did so, relentlessly driving his pen for the rest of a life that some thought shortened by the intensity of his labor.

After his marriage to Bessie Berdan, beautiful socialite daughter of an American admiral, he moved with his bride into a splendid villa in Sorrento, perched on a high cliff overlooking the Mediterranean, where they raised a family and took an active part in the civic life of the community. Crawford's particular diversion was sailing; he owned a seventy-five-foot schooner, the *Alden*, in which he crossed the Atlantic, navigating himself and sharing the work of the crew. His way of life excited the admiration of his friend Henry James, who described it to Hugh Walpole.

> James gave me a magnificent picture of that splendid figure, romantic in all his gestures, so handsome and vigorous, driving his boats fearlessly into the most dangerous seas, building his palaces on the Mediterranean shore, travelling over every corner of the globe, fearless and challenging and heroic.

But if James liked Crawford as a man and envied him his book sales, he had no wish to emulate him as a writer. In

1884 he had found Crawford's *To Leeward* "so contemptibly bad and ignoble that the idea of people reading it in such numbers makes one return upon oneself and ask what is the use of trying to write anything decent or serious for a public so absolutely idiotic." And nine years later he was writing to Robert Louis Stevenson: "I can't go with you three yards in your toleration either of Rider Haggard or Marion Crawford. Let me add that I can't read them, so I don't know anything about them."

This is the attitude of a literary high priest who has no use for aught but masterpieces at the altar. Crawford's half-sister, Mrs. Chanler, an erudite and exquisitely cultivated appreciator of music, art and letters, and herself a friend of both James and Edith Wharton, was far more temperate in her assessment, twenty-five years after her brother's death, of his work.

> He wrote very fast, sometimes as much as a chapter a day, covering sheet after sheet of foolscap with his neat scholarly characters; never a blot or an erasure. He had none of the tormenting doubt of self-criticism. Working hard and conscientiously, he had confidence in his work and saw no reason to think that by doing it over he might do it better. This gave his pages a certain freshness. His books were extremely successful — to this the publishers' checks bore witness.
>
> His pictures of Roman society in the mid-nineteenth century make pleasant reading even now [1934]. They are drawn from life as he saw it in those romantic years. The psychology is simple; there are good women and bad, always plainly labeled, and men of the highest courage and moral integrity opposed by unscrupulous villains.

The charm of his writing lay above all in his excellent gift of story-telling, and also in the great variety of settings and conditions in which his scenes were laid.

Note what Mrs. Chanler says about his pictures of *Roman* society. Crawford's many attempts to move his novel settings away from Italy were never so successful as his depictions of the land of his birth. *The Ralstons* and *Katherine Lauderdale*, dealing with fashionable New York of the 1890s, have none of the dash or verve of the Roman tales: Fifth Avenue will not convert to the Corso. One could scarcely imagine an early morning duel after a ball in Central Park, and without the duel, or at least the threat of one, much of the thrill of a Crawford novel subsides.

No, it was the Rome of his youth that always enchanted him, the Rome of Pio Nono and Cardinal Antonelli, of the French troops and the old "black" nobility who fought for the temporal power, of ancient titles and crumbling castles and dark intrigue, of beauty and passion, of cruelty and greed and superstition. I grant that Crawford muddies his books with the overcomplicated schemes of his villains, that his "good" women are too good and that his language, at emotional moments, soars to bathos, but his men are vivid and their deeds picturesque, and his Rome is as beautiful and unspoiled as Hawthorne's in *The Marble Faun*. Indeed, it is the same Rome.

I offer a single sample from one of the Roman novels to give a taste of Crawford at his best. *Pietro Ghisleri* is peopled with several of the characters from the *Saracinesca* trio. Its eponymous hero is a disillusioned romantic, with some as-pects of the Byronic lover. He is a bachelor in his early thir-ties with a crumbling castle in the country, a flat in Rome and an impeccable social position, owing to his ancient name, extreme good looks, exquisite manners and the reputation of being one of the best shots and swordsmen in the city. But Ghisleri has been deeply in love once and does not believe it can happen again; his adored one, a married woman, has died years before. He is sardonic and cynical; he has had affairs and duels; his life is considered by society to have been one of pardonable dissipation. His current mistress is the most beautiful woman in Rome, and her husband welcomes the distraction Ghisleri offers her from his own adulteries. Ghisleri is gallant and punctilious with his countess, but he can never convince her that he loves her as she does him, and she soon suspects that he is becoming, though unaware of it himself, fatally attracted to the lovely and virtuous English wife of Lord Herbert Arden, a cripple, who is his closest friend.

It can readily be seen that Crawford has created a hero irresistible to contemporary readers of sentimental fiction: a man with a reputation for wildness who is a model of deportment in the drawing room, a feared duellist whose lips hardly touch the back of the lady's hand that he raises gracefully to them. The reader knows that Lady Herbert will heal his broken heart and that they will marry happily when her crippled husband dies.

Then why isn't it mush? Because Pietro Ghisleri and Lady Herbert are so much alive. Crawford skillfully converts Lady Herbert's horror at being attracted to her husband's best friend into an actual dislike of him, which Ghisleri eventually overcomes by accepting it. When they come together at last it is sudden, but we know that its suddenness is caused by the fact that their love grew to maturity in unawareness.

I quote one scene to give an example of the tenseness that Crawford knew so well how to create. A group of gentlemen at a club are discussing the incident of Lord Herbert's having fainted at a ball. Lady Herbert's wicked sister, Adele Savelli, has circulated a rumor that this was caused by drink and that Lord Herbert is in fact a confirmed alcoholic. Incidentally, malicious gossip in Roman society in Crawford's novels is invariably not only completely unfounded but universally believed. The clubmen in this instance are no exception.

Unfortunately for one of them who happened to be declaiming on the subject, but who was really by no means a bad fellow, he did not notice that Ghisleri had entered the room before he had finished his speech. When he had quite done, Ghisleri came forward.

"Arden is my old friend," he said quietly. "He never drinks. He has a disease of the heart and he fainted from the heat. The doctor and I took him home together. I hope that none of you will take up this disgusting story which was started by the women. And I hope Pietresanta there will do me the honor to believe what I say, and to tell you that he was mistaken."

Ghisleri was not a pleasant person to quarrel with, and moreover had the reputation of being truthful. His story, too, was quite as probable as the other, to say the least of it. Don Gianbattista Pietresanta glanced quickly from one to the other of the men who were seated around him as though to ask their advice in the matter. Several of them nodded, almost imperceptibly, as though counselling him to do as Ghisleri requested. There was nothing at all aggressive in the latter's manner, either, as he quietly lit a cigarette while waiting for the other's answer . . .

Pietresanta was neither stupid nor bad, and he was not a coward.

"I do not know Lord Herbert Arden myself," he said without affectation. "What I said I got on hearsay, and the whole story is evidently a fabrication which we ought to deny. For the rest, Ghisleri, if you are not quite satisfied —" He stopped and looked at Pietro.

"My dear fellow," said the latter, "what more could I have to say about the affair? You all seemed to be in the dark, and I wanted to clear the matter up for the sake of my old friend. That is all. I am very much obliged to you."

The small crisis has been well handled, but every man in that chamber knew how it might have ended: as does another, a few chapters later, when Ghisleri lies close to death on the field of honor with a bullet through one lung.

Crawford, as already noted, was a student at Saint Paul's School, and the library there has a room devoted to the publications of its graduates. As I gazed on a visit at the shelves of Crawford titles, all in gleamingly mint first editions, now so little read, the words of Ivy Compton-Burnett on Agatha Christie came back to me: "Think of the pleasure she must give — think of the pleasure!" And I like to think of the pleasure he gave.

HAROLD FREDERIC

❧ ❧ ❧

H AROLD FREDERIC (1856–1898) packed a great deal
into the forty-two years of his life. He wrote several successful volumes of fiction and nonfiction; he attained wide
fame as an international journalist; and he became a political
adviser to Grover Cleveland when the latter was governor of
New York. He was a brilliant and lively conversationalist and
made good friends among prominent statesmen and writers
in America and England, in which latter country he spent the
last decade of his life. Yet he is remembered today for a single
novel, *The Damnation of Theron Ware*.

He was born in Utica, New York, and raised in very modest circumstances by a strict and stalwart fundamentalist
Methodist mother, who was widowed when Frederic was an
infant. He ran off to Boston when still in his teens to lead a
bohemian life as a writer, painter and photo-retoucher. When
he had decided that writing was to be his career, he returned
to Utica and found a job on the staff of *The Observer*. Success
came early to him: his articles gained a wide readership,
enabling him to write and publish short stories and to marry
and start a family. When he moved to Albany, partly at the
persuasion of a Catholic priest, who helped to wean him from
Methodism without converting him to Rome, he managed to

secure a post as editor of *The Republican Evening Journal* despite his tender age of twenty-seven and his decidedly liberal views.

When Cleveland became governor in 1883, Frederic found himself welcome at the gubernatorial mansion. As Allan Nevins wrote in his life of the twenty-second and twenty-fourth president: "Frederic's wit and cultivation appealed to Cleveland as a welcome change from the shoals of politicians . . . Versatile, light-hearted, full of ideas, his talk diverted the governor while his editorials were among the few which Cleveland read."

When Cleveland was nominated as the Democratic candidate for the presidency in 1884, Frederic's enthusiasm knew no bounds. He wrote to him that he felt at last like a proud Roman citizen. America needed no longer to ape foreign countries or "seek dishonored wealth to win class distinction and the idleness of the aristocrat in older countries." A new age was dawning, he exclaimed, and "as in a burst of sunlight, the pride of country, of race, yes, of state, comes to me now, and I am almost intoxicated by its radiance and power." There *was* a public conscience, after all, he went on, and "all the greed and scoundrelism and folly of our political, race and business sides, massed in one grand desperate effort for control, are not able to stand before the simple weight of an honest man and an upright cause!"

To which the future president could only reply warmly: "There *is* a God!"

Frederic published his second best novel, *Seth's Brother's Wife*, in 1887, the only one of his fictions that can even compare with his masterpiece. It is the story of a young farmer in upper New York who is almost seduced by the wife of his older brother, a crooked politician, and who is so abashed when confronted with this dalliance by the latter that he agrees to support his candidature for Congress though it is opposed to everything he stands for. The book, like some others of Frederic, is full of confused moral standards, and reflects the reporter in him who could not help seeing too many points of view. But the vagaries and complexities of the plot are in part compensated for by the vividness of the descriptions and character delineations. Here is Frederic on one of his favorite themes, the poverty of American rural life:

> The American farm-house funeral is surely, of all the observances with which civilized man marks the end of this earthly pilgrimage, the most pathetic. The rural life itself is a sad and sterile enough thing, with its unrelieved physical strain, its enervating and destructive diet, its mental barrenness, its sternly narrowed groove of toil and thought and companionship — but death at the farm brings a desolating gloom, a cruel sense of the hopelessness of existence, which one realizes nowhere else.

Frederic's liberal views in the Cleveland campaign cost him his job on the Albany paper, and he moved to England as a *New York Times* correspondent. There, he attained a wide following, covering the cholera epidemic in southern Europe, riots and border wars, and threw himself wholeheartedly into the Irish Home Rule movement. He even wrote a full-length book on the young Kaiser Wilhelm II, which began by shrewdly assessing the vanity and pugnacity of his nature, but ended with an optimistic estimate of his maturing character, which history, alas, was not to bear out.

In *The Damnation of Theron Ware* (1896), which is quite unlike any of his other books, Frederic addresses himself to the bewilderment and ultimate absurdity of a semi-educated American would-be idealist struggling in the arid culture of a northern

New York State small town towards the end of the nineteenth century. Theron Ware is a Methodist minister of limited intelligence, and of a small but fanciful imagination and a faith in his own stagy preaching that he would rather ascribe to God than to his own vanity — in short, a very average man. A character in one of Ivy Compton-Burnett's novels, responding to the comment that most people must be average, or there would not be such a thing, remarks, "Well, let us hope there is not." Frederic's protagonist makes us echo this.

What Frederic was really doing was blazing a trail that Sinclair Lewis was to follow in *Main Street* and *Babbitt*: describing the effect on a shallow but vaguely aspiring mind of a culture dominated by querulous and bigoted religious sects and pseudo-patriotic fraternities. Henry James had incurred the wrath of his compatriots by deploring the lack in Nathaniel Hawthorne's America of any of the great stabilizing, unifying traditions of old Europe, such as an established church or monarchy or social hierarchy, something to give shape and coherence to any given society. The United States had come a long way from Hawthorne, but in the eighteen-eighties and -nineties the hinterlands had still much of their old flavor. And Theron Ware is ultimately rejected by the only three intellectuals in the whole town of Octavius, not because he has vainly tried to become one of them, and not even because he has done it so sneakily, but because he bores them. It is a great tribute to the author's skillful prose that he does not bore us.

It is Ware's misfortune, if not his tragedy, that he is assigned to a town where the Methodists are at their most evangelical and meanest, untouched by the softer doctrines already then sponsored in larger communities. His long-suffering wife, Alice, must remove the flowers from her hat, and he is cautioned by the stingy hypocritical trustees of the dismal, organless, choirless church to use no fancy words in his sermons but to emphasize the burning threat of hell fire.

Frederic's description of the senior trustee, Brother Pierce, might have been written by the reminiscing Henry James of *Notes of a Son and Brother*:

> The irregular thin-lipped mouth, slightly sunken, and shut with vice-like firmness, the short snub nose, and the little eyes squinting from half-closed lids beneath slightly marked brows, seemed scarcely to attain to the dignity of features, but evaded attention instead, as if feeling that they were only there at all from plain necessity, and ought not to be taken into account. Mr. Pierce's face did not know how to smile — what was the use of smiles? — but its whole surface radiated secretiveness.

And here is how Henry James described a professor at Harvard Law School, of about the same period, who not only drove him from that profession, but may have contributed to his ultimate emigration:

> Of the third of our instructors, I mainly recall that he represented dryness and hardness, prose unrelieved, at their deadliness — partly perhaps because he was most master of his subject. He was nonetheless placeable for these things withal, and what mainly comes back to me of him was the full sufficiency with which he made me ask myself how I *could* for a moment have seen myself really browse in any field where the marks of the shepherd were such an oblong dome of a bare cranium, such a fringe of dropping little ringlets toward its base, and a mouth so meanly retentive, so ignorant of style as I made out, above a chin so

indifferent to the duty, or at least to the opportunity of chins.

Ware calls on Father Forbes, the local Catholic priest, and finds him enjoying a succulent meal, with wine, in the company of a brilliant atheist doctor, Ledsman, and he gleans from their witty and learned discourse that he not only knows nothing about the Catholic Church, but nothing about biblical history; indeed, nothing about history itself.

Ware learns about Catholics as his creator learned about them from the Catholic priest friend in Albany. As one character tells him: "You do not realize that they are held up by the power of the true church, as a little child learning to walk is held up with a belt by its nurse. They can say and do things, and no harm will come to them which would mean destruction to you because they have help and you are walking alone."

Nothing was clearer to his [Ware's] mind than the conclusion itself — that his meeting with the priest and the doctor was the turning point in his career. They had lifted him bodily out of the slough of ignorance, of contact with low minds, and put him on solid ground . . . Evidently there was an intellectual world, a world of culture and grace, of lofty thoughts and the inspiring communion of real knowledge, where creeds were not of importance, and where men asked one another, not "Is your soul saved?" but "Is your mind well furnished?" Theron had the sensation of having been invited to become a citizen of this world.

Ware at once repudiates his past. He will no longer feel bound to sacrifice himself to a notion of duty to "those low-minded and coarse-natured villagers." He will turn his back on the miserable "combination of hypocrisy and hysterics which they called their spiritual life." And this, the author appears to be telling us, is the beginning of Ware's damnation. Why? Because the thought of becoming a citizen of this new world "so dazzled him that his impulses were dragging him forward to take the new oath of allegiance before he had had time to reflect upon what it was he was abandoning."

This, perhaps a bit disappointingly, is the crux of the novel. There *is*, according to Frederic, though he never permits us more than a glimpse of it, *some* good in the old-fashioned Bible-thumping Methodism, or at least some good in the benighted souls who have nothing but it to turn to. He expresses this point of view meagerly through Sister Soulsby, a tough, realistic but kindly woman who has been through the toughest mills of life and emerged as a noisy but effective church fund raiser. She sees that Ware is about to tumble between two stools and tries to settle him back on the old one, but it is in vain. He is committed to romp on down his primrose path.

Ware now fancies himself in love with the local Catholic heiress, Celia Madden, an irresponsible, red-headed, intellectual, free-thinking beauty who is only playing with him. He sees his devoted but less interesting wife as a burden with which he has been shackled in the ignorance of his youth, and he plans to ditch not only her but his church and elope to a new life supported by Celia's riches. The latter's gold enhances her charms:

> The glamour of a separate banking account shone upon her. Where the soft woodland light played in among the strands of her disordered hair, he saw the veritable gleam of gold. A mysterious new suggestion of power blended

itself with the beauty of her face, was exhaled in the faint perfume of her garments.

Ware now sinks to his lowest point. He professes to believe that his wife's acceptance of gifts of expensive flowers for her garden from a neighboring bachelor lawyer is evidence of an amatory intrigue, thus building an excuse for leaving her. The lawyer expresses the reader's opinion when he tells an acquaintance:

> "I've just been talking to a man who's so much meaner than any other man I ever heard of that it takes my breath away. He's got a wife that's as pure and good as gold, and he knows it, and she worships the ground he walks on, and he knows that too. And yet the scoundrel is going around trying to sniff out some shadow of a pretext for misusing her worse than he's ever done."

Of course Ware's schemes come to nothing, and it is Sister Soulsby who saves the broke ex-minister by sending him and his still faithful wife to a real estate job in Seattle. But we know he will find only further hell there, for he has learned nothing, not even to appreciate the wife he has so misused. In the end he is indulging in the fantasy that his gift as a preacher may be converted into the foundation of a successful political career.

> There rose before his fancy, out of the chaos of these shapeless imaginings, some faces of men, then more of them, then a great concourse of uplifted countenances, crowded close together as far as the eye could reach. They were attentive faces all, rapt, eager, credulous to a degree.

Their eyes were admiringly bent upon a common object of excited interest. They were looking at *him*; they strained their ears to miss no cadence of his voice. Involuntarily he straightened himself, stretched forth his hand with the pale thin fingers gracefully disposed, and passed it slowly before him from side to side, in a comprehensive, stately gesture. The audience rose at him, as he dropped his hand, and filled his daydream with a mighty roar of applause, in volume like an ocean tempest, yet pitched for his hearing alone.

The miracle of the novel is that a character as spineless and vain as Ware can sustain a reader's interest, but, like Babbitt, he can. Frederic, as indicated, was a great reporter, and it may have helped him to see his native land from the perspective of England, where he had lived so long. Not that, like Henry James, he was an admirer of English hierarchies and traditions. In *Gloria Mundi*, the story of an English lad who in Anthony Hope's Graustarkian manner finds himself unexpectedly the heir of an ancient dukedom, Frederic goes out of his way to explore everything that is rotten in the British caste system, but at the same time, being a good reporter, he allows his hero to benefit from a sense of inherited *noblesse oblige*. There is no such remedy for Theron Ware.

Stanton Garner fitted *The Damnation* neatly into its proper niche in American fiction when he wrote that it "presents not only a brilliantly conceived and fascinating protagonist but a representative but unpromising man at the end of an era of confidence and simple faith and the beginning of a darker era of complexity and doubt."

The last chapter of Frederic's short life is told in Leon Edel's biography of Henry James. He had left his wife and was raising another family with his mistress, Kitty Lyon, in a house he had taken to be near his friend Stephen Crane, in the neighborhood of Rye, where James lived.

Crane's friend Harold Frederic, a fellow-American and London correspondent of the *New York Times*, took a less generous view of the rituals of the master. A down-to-earth, rough and ready newspaper man . . . he characterized James as "an effeminate old donkey who lives with a herd of other donkeys around him and insists on being treated as if he were the Pope." And he spoke of James's "usual lack of a sense of generosity." Both Crane and Frederic lived "hard" and died young — Frederic of a stroke that very year, at forty-two. He had maintained two households and left legitimate as well as illegitimate children. He would have been astonished to learn that the man he described as lacking generosity was among the first to sign an appeal for money for his [Frederic's] illegitimate children . . . He [James] had chronicled the lives of dissolute artists in his novels and tales. If he passed judgment on them, it was not that they led bohemian lives but that they made their bohemianism an excuse for poor art. When Cora Crane sent Frederic's posthumous work, *The Market Place*, to the Master, he read it with "a lively sense of what Harold Frederic might have done if he had lived (and therefore worked) differently."

Paul Hervieu

᷒ᘐ ᷒ᘐ ᷒ᘐ

T HE COURSE THAT I TOOK at Yale, in 1938, which has
most stayed with me in the long aftermath was Joseph
Seronde's in nineteenth-century French drama and fiction.
That rich field, with a few exceptions in Dumas and Hugo,
was then virgin territory to me, but it had an immediate and
powerful influence on my reading and writing that has lasted
to this day. Indeed, I was one day to write a novel, *A World of
Profit*, whose plot was extricated, without even an acknowledgment, from the Goncourt brothers' *Renée Mauperin*. No critic
noticed.

One author who figured in both the plays and the novels
of the course was Paul Hervieu (1857–1915), in whose work I
took particular delight. Although little known in America and
now largely forgotten in France, he had a great following
in his day, and George Painter, in the index "Persons and
Places" to his biography of Marcel Proust, lists him as one of
the several possible models not only for Bergotte but for
Swann. For Hervieu was as well known to the literary as to
the fashionable world of the *belle époque*.

As a young man he studied but never practiced law, and
served briefly in the diplomatic corps before giving it up to

devote himself to literature, on what were apparently adequate private means. He became a regular diner-out, cultivating political, social and artistic circles, like the young Henry James in London and the young Proust in Paris, in an avid quest of subject material for his stories and dramas. We catch a glimpse of him in 1887 in the journal of Edmond de Goncourt: "A little youth, distinguished, pretty, with the sweet manner of a scion of good society who has been tutored by an abbé . . . he talks curiously, with individual ideas, of literature." Fernand Gregh noted his rather frigid appearance and that he seemed to have "little icicles in the corners of his moustache."

Two years later Goncourt refers to a love affair, disapproved of by Hervieu's family, that has brought the unhappy young man to the verge of suicide. The reference is undoubtedly to the Baronne Marguerite de Pierrebourg, a charming and intellectual society lady, separated from her husband, who was also a writer and kept a brilliant salon. The affair survived whatever crisis the journal refers to and lasted happily for the next twenty-five years, ending only with Hervieu's death. Painter believes that it suggested to Proust the relationship between Swann and Odette, though that ended in marriage. At any rate Proust wrote to Madame de Pierrebourg when Hervieu died that they had lost a great friend and a great writer. He almost forgave the deceased for having voted in 1914 against granting the French Academy's award to *Du Côté de Chez Swann*.

It is pleasant to note in passing that Hervieu, in a society of violent anti-Semitism, was an active Dreyfusard.

Of his dramas only one remains still read at all, *La Course du Flambeau*, and of his novels two, *Peints par Eux-mêmes* and *L'Armature*. The play, which was a popular vehicle for Réjane, deals with three generations of women. Sabine Revel believes in the beginning that she loves her mother and her daughter equally, but when the latter's husband fails in business and his desperate wife goes after her grandmother's capital, which the old lady is stubbornly preserving for Sabine, a terrible conflict ensues, in which Sabine will ultimately sacrifice her mother's health and very life for her greedy child's sake, allowing her to take the now ailing granddaughter to a climate that will be fatal to the grandmother's heart. In the end, having lost the man she loves and been abandoned by the daughter for whom she has sold her soul, Sabine can only exclaim over her mother's corpse, tearing her hand from the dead woman's grip: "How she clutches me! And her eyes! Dead! She's dead! For my daughter I've killed my mother!"

The excitement and tenseness of the play arise from the audience's indignation at the complete willingness of Sabine's odious daughter to sacrifice both her mother and grandmother for the sake of her bungling, grabbing spouse, and the pathetic struggle that Sabine's old mother puts up to keep her daughter from ruining herself in her obsession with her only child.

Peints par Eux-mêmes is an epistolary novel and a very successful one: each letter writer has his or her particular style. It is made up of letters written by and to the members of a house party given by the Comte and Comtesse de Pontarmé in their splendid but gloomy old castle in Indre-et-Loire. The hostess writes benignly but pompously; her daughter, unhappily separated from her husband, sentimentally and self-pityingly; the portrait painter, of a different social milieu, trenchantly and wittily; and the smoothly handsome Italian prince, courting the heiress daughter of the parvenu ogre Baron Munstein and informing his distinguished but impecunious father of his financial prospects, coldly and lucidly. The total correspondence constitutes a lively if appalling picture of an idle and *désoeuvré* (except for Munstein and the painter) society, with little to do but chase the stag, seduce one's neighbor's wife and be ever on the alert to acquire the money needed to maintain one's inherited rank by any means other than honest work.

Success is represented by the Italian prince, Silvère de Carean. He knows precisely what he is worth to the great boor Munstein, whom he inwardly despises, and will not settle for a penny less. He assesses the virtues of the latter's daughter exactly: she possesses, despite her parentage, the looks, the bearing and the education for the station to which marriage with the prince will raise her, and the bodily attractions to satisfy him, for a time, anyway, long enough to ensure the continuance of his line in the Almanach de Gotha. And her dowry must be settled in such a way as to leave him at liberty to drop the acquaintance of his vulgar in-laws should they ever get in his way. The prince's father is something of a dreamer, an old-timer; the son, who is sophisticated in modern economic arrangements, will take care of everything, including the welfare of his siblings, who are as broke as himself. The rescue of an ancient family with the money bags of an international swindler will contribute to the stabilization of society — such as it is. It works for the moment, anyway.

Failure in the castle is represented by Françoise de Trémeur. She is unhappily married to a rich but unsympathetic nobleman and passionately in love with a young wastrel and gambler, "Glé-Glé" Le Hinglé, of good family but poor, whose only virtue seems to lie in his total reciprocation of her devotion. She has been too sensitive and refined to continue sexual relations with her husband while she is Le Hinglé's mistress, with the terrifying result that she is now in no position to ascribe to her spouse the unwanted pregnancy she has suddenly discovered. In terror that the latter may kill her if he finds out, and maybe kill her lover as well, she undergoes an abortion, but it is her misfortune to have the letter in which she relates this fall into the hands of Munstein.

The baron takes full advantage of this windfall. He informs Françoise that she can retrieve the letter only by submitting to his lust; otherwise, it will be sent to her husband. He is such a monster that he actually prefers his victims to hate him; sex to him is a species of rape. There is a note in Edmond de Goncourt's journal about how Hervieu, in speaking of one Bischoffsheim, who had boasted that he could have any society lady he wanted for a thousand francs, had exclaimed: "These creatures soil everything they touch!" Perhaps this was the moment of birth for Baron Munstein, and also for Baron Saffre of *L'Armature.*

Françoise alerts her lover to her danger, and Le Hinglé lures the baron to a supposed rendezvous with her and then presents himself, revolver in hand, ready to kill Munstein if he will not hand over the incriminating document. Munstein hesitates. Will Le Hinglé really risk the guillotine to get it? But Françoise's lover replies (as he writes in his final letter to her) that he has no fear of reprisals, as he plans in any event to kill himself that same day. He has been caught cheating at cards at his club, and none of his acquaintances will ever speak to him again. His life is over, or will be as soon as he has restored the document to Françoise. Munstein believes him, hands it over and leaves. And then Le Hinglé finishes his epistle:

> And now, my love, you must know that what I told that man was true . . . We will have loved each other without remorse, like two wild beasts, with passion. But we have

always known the social conventions held us in their grip. And tonight it is my turn to die, in the cage, turning a long last look on you. And you must watch me without a twitch, without a word, without even seeming to take it in, like a lioness.

But Françoise does not take it like a lioness; she kills herself with an overdose. Her pathetic love story is surely the finest thing in all of Hervieu. The glimpses we have of her from the other correspondents all add to our sense of her charm; everyone is drawn to her, even her frustrated husband. She may be caught, like Phèdre, in the talons of a relentless Venus, but she still has moments of exquisite delight in writing to her absent lover and recalling the joy of their meetings, even at times when she is trembling with panic at the idea of what her husband might do if he learns about them. She can even take brief comfort in the pregnancy that her adored one has caused — even when she knows it must be aborted. And she is at her most pitiable when imploring Le Hinglé to avoid gambling, yet admitting that if the alternative is to be other women, she would consent to his ruin at baccarat. Hervieu conveys the sense of a lovely creature crushed by a society with which, for all her cleverness and skill, she cannot ultimately cope, with the same vividness of Edith Wharton's depiction of Lily Bart in *The House of Mirth*.

L'Armature is a more dramatic novel — or more melodramatic — than its predecessor and sold thirty thousand copies, a prodigious figure for the 1890s, but the violence of its sermonizing and the extremities to which the characters stretch their vices tell against it on a reading a century later. The central thesis that money is the scaffolding which upholds society and provides the basic motive for every human action is heavily and constantly underlined: the villain Munstein of the earlier novel has become even more monstrous as the Baron Saffre, who frustrates the revenge of the business associate for whose advancement a loving wife has sacrificed her virtue to the ogre, by suffering a paralyzing stroke, so that the cuckold can only spit helplessly in the helpless invalid's face.

Saffre's children are not much better than their sire. The lovely Comtesse de Grommelain takes on lover after lover between doses of morphine and amuses herself by writing informative anonymous letters to ignorant cuckolds of Parisian society. Her sister, Madame Bréhand, a rolling mass of obesity, uses her fortune to keep her penniless and would-be-philanderer husband on a short strict leash. He trembles at the idea that a single misstep would put him in the street. All of the characters, except for the baron's wife, who operates in the end as a kind of *dea ex machina* to save her offspring from moral and financial ruin, and the couple whose marriage he has violated, are despicably selfish and greedy.

The author may, however, have a gleam of sympathy for the baron's daughter-in-law, Catherine Saffre, who rejects adultery as the antidote to a loveless marriage out of an inherent sense of decency and *noblesse oblige*. Her noble family has sold her, and she feels herself bound by the bargain in which she participated.

Indeed, perhaps the best thing in the novel — which, for all its sensationalism, is immensely readable — is the understanding and sympathy between Catherine Saffre and her brother-in-law, the Comte de Grommelain. Both are of ancient lineage; both are aware of how deeply they have compromised themselves in a money marriage. He has saved his line from bastardy by denying his wife, after the birth of two sons whose paternity he has no reason to doubt, all further marital relations. She must now watch herself in her adulteries. Furthermore, as soon as he is sure of a family inheritance of his own, he plans to have his lawyer catch her in *flagrante delicto* and demand a separation. In his and Catherine's conversations they are like two kindred souls shipwrecked on an odiously comfortable isle. One can see why Proust so admired Hervieu's treatment of the "old faubourg." It is not unlike his own.

ROBERT HERRICK

※ ※ ※

D ANIEL AARON, in his sensitive and perceptive introduction to the Harvard University Press's 1962 reissue of Herrick's *The Memoirs of an American Citizen*, quotes from a letter of George Santayana, in which the philosopher-poet pictures certain of his old Harvard friends, in particular the poets George Cabot Lodge, Trumbull Stickney and William Vaughn Moody, as trying to cope with the barren materials of American life:

> . . . but every day their own talent grew thinner and ghostlier, and the subject matter which American life offered them — when not treated (as it is now-a-days) satirically — was woefully stifled and starved. In the 1890s or thereabouts, I knew half a dozen young Harvard poets, Moody being the most successful of them with the public: every one of them was simply killed, snuffed out by the environment. They hadn't enough stamina to stand up to their country and describe it as a poet could. It was not that they imitated the English — they were ferocious anglophobes — but that, being educated men, they couldn't pitch their voices or find their inspiration in that strident society.

Among those young men whom Santayana knew and taught, however, was one who not only escaped the Boston sterility that the master deplored, but who certainly learned to pitch his voice — at times even shrilly — in the strident society that he discovered in the Middle West: Robert Herrick (1868–1938). Herrick had moved to Chicago, where he lived (or "camped," as Aaron puts it) for thirty years, teaching English and composition at the University of Chicago, "holding himself aloof from his students, to whom he lectured with averted face," and pouring out in novel after novel his New Englandish, Hawthornian moral indignation at the greed, corruption and materialism of the Windy City. He wrote in 1895 to William Dean Howells, who had early noted and published him:

> Really I write about this town neither because I like it or hate it, but because I can't escape it and because I am so ashamed of it. If you are condemned to residence on a muckheap, wouldn't you too edit it? Wouldn't you want to give it some credit, some standing (*as* a muckheap) by ordering, formulating, characterizing its various delectabilities? No — I am only devoting Chicago to literary manipulation ... to raise this dirt pile to some dignity ... by annexing it to the principality of literature.

Herrick's genealogy on both sides was of old Massachusetts colonial stock, traceably related to some currently prominent families, but his father's folk had been poor farmers, and his mother, a bitter, self-centered woman, if her proposed prototype in his novel *Waste* is a fair portrait, soured the home with her obsession that she had married beneath her. Herrick had somehow scraped together the money needed to matriculate at Harvard, where he escaped to the love of literature and the arts and to the cultivation of such intellectual friends as George Pierce Baker, Bernard Berenson and Norman Hapgood. He married, too young, a cousin — the match ended in bitter divorce — taught English for three years at the Massachusetts Insitute of Technology, and moved west. His emulation of the fiction of such French realist writers as Flaubert, Bourget and Zola was to stand him in good stead in his depiction of life in Chicago.

Let me state here that in my opinion the only novel in Herrick's canon that is worth reading today is *The Memoirs of an American Citizen* (1905). But before discussing this remarkable book, it is only fair to point out that Herrick had a good deal to say to his contemporaries, and that he said some of it very well.

Like Edith Wharton and Robert Grant, he was very much alive to the problems presented to upper-middle-class American wives by a life of leisure (household work had been taken over by immigrants), for which they had neither the education nor the training. As he put it in *The Common Lot* (1904):

> Their husbands, working furiously here in the resounding city, maintained them in luxury for their relaxation and amusement, and, provided they kept on the broad avenues of married life, cared little how they spent their days. In Steele's great store, and in a thousand other stores and factories of the vast city, girls and women were mechanically pounding their machines hour after hour. The fine flower of all their dead labor in life was the luxury of these women.

Religion no longer provided a refuge or an occupation for these pampered females; a typical one finds "that the colorless Protestantism of her fathers had faded into a nameless moralism." Helen, the heroine of the novel, who is married to a brilliant but unscrupulous architect, seeing him succumb to the temptation of building shoddy houses in sweetheart deals with greedy contractors, can at first only conceive this hope: "Surely a new order of the world was to be born wherein the glory of life should not be for the ferocious self-seekers."

Only towards the end of the book does she undergo a deeper change of heart. "From a soft, yielding dreaming feminine thing there was born a new soul — definite, hard and precise in its judgment of men and life."

When her husband, at last relenting at the sight of one of his firetraps burning up, with a terrible loss of life, makes a full confession at a public hearing, she and he embark on a new existence. But the author's essential cynicism is frankly stated in the paragraph where he explains why the architect escapes with only a fine and no jail sentence.

In *Together* (1908) Herrick allows himself to speculate whether some essential vigor has not been lost, not only by the women, but by the men in this money-obsessed culture. His character Margaret Pole feels free to betray though not to repudiate her weak husband. She "can endure vice and folly and disappointment, but not a petty, trivial, chattering biped masquerading as a man." And a male character, a doctor, exclaims: "Great God! I had rather those broad-hipped Italian peasant women of Calabria, with solid, red-brown flesh, bred bastards for the country than have these thin anaemic nervous sexless creatures, with their 'souls' and their 'charm,' marry and become mothers!"

The heroine, Isabel Price, hearing this diatribe, feels all her past ambitions shrivel into petty nothings. There is nothing left for her to do with her life but go back to the husband who has driven her, with his boring business obsessions, to live apart. A fidelity to an incompatible marriage seems the only virtue open to Herrick's unhappy women. But he certainly saw that this society had to be basically altered.

The plight of the woman soon became the plight of the man who, by the very nature of the problem, was bound to become her victim. If a woman, trained for nothing socially useful but the bearing of children (and Herrick's women have often almost lost this function), must find the money on which to live — and to live well — where can she get it but from a man? And if that man has the ambition and desire to do something useful in this world (besides earning money), such as making an important scientific discovery or producing a work of art, he will have to sacrifice his noble aim in order to support a household and to privately educate his children. The vicious grip in which the sexes hold themselves is graphically described in *One Woman's Life* (1913).

Milly Ridge, the heroine, belongs "to the class too proud to take charity and too incompetent to earn money." She exclaims: "I have no gifts; I was never clever with books. I like life, people!" And then she stretches out her hands gropingly to the broad horizon. Her husband sacrifices a real painter's talent to support her, inadequately, as the illustrator of popular novels and dies of heart disease brought on by overwork and frustration. Milly, looking at the one good picture he had ever done, realizes that he had been in pursuit of something that she can never understand. "Naturally Milly did not analyze closely her own troubled mind. Here was plain evidence of her husband's being in which she no longer had the smallest share."

Herrick's conclusion puts the final blame on the men. "Milly was the type of which men through the ages, in their paramount desire for exclusive sex possession, had made of women, what civilization made of her, and society still encouraged her to become when she could — an adventuress . . . a fortuitous, somewhat parasitic creature."

Herrick's novels grew steadily longer and angrier. He would introduce new characters fatiguingly and then kill them off unexpectedly, and his descriptions of country landscapes and interiors became overdetailed. His fiction seemed at last to justify the term that Henry James unfairly applied to the masterpieces of the Russians: "fluid puddings." His only consistency was his constant rage against the evils of American capitalism. Yet he produced one masterpiece, *The Memoirs of an American Citizen.* How did he do it?

Very simply. In two ways. First, he managed for once to control the point of view. Van Harrington, the narrator or memoirist, tells his story in his own words. This in a stroke eliminates Herrick's peculiar stumbling block: his inability to unite into any kind of artistic whole the points of view of his large casts of characters with his own authorial overview. Second, his narrator himself is a greedy capitalist and is thus barred from using any of his creator's usual diatribes against the order.

Readers are always peeking behind fictional characters to seek out the human model they feel the author must have been copying. Often it is the author himself, even if the character is a villain. There are critics who have seen Henry James behind Gilbert Osmond, the heartless dilettante of *The Portrait of a Lady*: the man he feared he *might* have become. And we know that Flaubert once exclaimed: *"Madame Bovary, c'est moi!"* I do not claim that Herrick saw himself in Van Harrington, but once a writer puts himself into an "I" character, once he starts acting the part, he begins in a fashion to take his side. And that is why *The Memoirs* is such a striking tour de force. Almost to its very end the reader has, if not a strong sympathy for the narrator, at least more sympathy for him than for the characters who seek to destroy him. It is only natural to "root" for an "I."

Harrington is born desperately poor in a poor Indiana town, of parents who care little for him. He learns a hard lesson about thievery when he is caught stealing apples from a mean old judge in the neighborhood.

> I came to the conclusion that if I wanted what my neighbor considered to be his, I must get the law to do the business for me. For the first time it dawned on me how wonderful is that system which shuts up one man for taking a few dollars' worth of truck that doesn't belong to him, and honors the man who steals his millions — if he robs in the legal way! Yes, the old judge knocked some good worldly sense into me.

Falsely accused of pickpocketing in a Chicago store, Harrington is released by a kindly but skeptical magistrate, who tells him to go back to Indiana, but, learning that the lad has come north to seek his fortune, lends him a dollar, with the warning that in "this glorious republic" it is "every man's first privilege to take his own road to hell." Harrington does so, but his road is, for the most part — as much as practicable — a legal one. As he asks himself: "What was there in Chicago in 1877 to live for but Success?"

Yet even Chicago had its own poetry, at least for Harrington.

> There's something pretty close to the earth in all of us, if we have the stomach to do the world's work: men of bone and sinew and rich blood, the strong men who do the deeds at the head of the ranks, feed close to the earth. The

lowing cattle in the pens, the squealing hogs in the cars, the smell of the fat carcasses in the heavy wagons drawn by the sleek Percherons — it all made me think of the soft, fertile fields from which we take the grain — the blood and flesh that enter into our being.

His rise to riches in the stockyards, from truck driving to sausage dealing to management in meat packing, is told forcefully and succinctly, for Harrington is not one to indulge in his creator's lavish descriptions. The reader finds himself backing the narrator in all his fights and deals, even when he begins to step across the line of the law, for in every case he is outwitting an even more unscrupulous opponent, who seeks to bankrupt him. When at last he stoops to bribing a judge, he forfeits the reader's sympathy, but even then his self-defense has a terrible force: that those who are too morally squeamish to fight with brass knuckles are doomed to be knocked out. "The strong must rule," he argues; "the world was for the strong. It was the act of an idiot to deny that truth."

When Harrington at last, though he has by now purchased a seat in the United States Senate, must face in his own heart the moral ruin he has brought on one of his associates in crime, we are deaf to his plea that he has done only what the other builders of the American economy have done:

In all the forty years of my life there has been no evil as I know evil. No man could say that he had had harm from me unless it might be poor Ed Hostetter — and for thousands of such workers as live from day to day, depending on men like me to give them their chance to earn bread for their wives and children, I had made the world better rather than worse. Unthinking thousands lived and had

children and got what good there was in life because of me
and my will.

But to others, the good ones, to Farson and Dround and
May, I was but a common thief, a criminal, who fattened
on the evil of the world. What had they done to make life?
What was their virtue good for? They took the dainty
paths and kept their clothes from the soil of the road.

One believes, however, in the sincerity of the misguided
memoirist. What is harder to believe is his statement that in
his early boarding-house days he pored over Darwin, Spen-
cer, Stubbs and Lecky at night. That, from a man who had
no formal education after the age of sixteen and spent his
long days in the stockyards, is hard to credit. Herrick has
gone a bit far.

The Great Depression of 1929 struck the now elderly but
increasingly radical Herrick as a judgment on greedy Americans, and he became a staunch supporter of the New Deal.
The Roosevelt administration appointed him government
secretary of the Virgin Islands, a post that he filled successfully for the three last years of his life.

Leon Edel, in the final volume of his life of Henry James,
The Master, offers this picture of his subject with Herrick on
his American tour in 1905:

> We get a glimpse of James in Chicago one day when he
> returns from a luncheon engagement on the far South Side
> by way of a suburban train, along the wintry shore of the
> lake, accompanied by Robert Herrick, the Chicago nov-
> elist. They ride through "the smudged purlieus of the
> untidy city into the black gloom of the Loop." James sits
> huddled on the dingy bench of the railway car, draped in
> the loose folds of his mackintosh, his hands clasped about

his baggy umbrella, "his face haggard under the shuttling blows of the Chicago panorama." "What monstrous ugliness!" he murmurs in a tone of pure physical anguish.

Herrick later sent James his latest novel, *The Common Lot*, apparently accompanied with a plea that the Master should not revise his own earlier works (as it was known James was planning) for the proposed Scribner edition of his fiction. But James was adamant in his courteous rejection of the suggestion: "Forgive me my blatant confidence in my own lucid literary sense."

There is no record of what the Master thought of Herrick's offered novel. Perhaps it is just as well.

Amy Lowell

ᴥ ᴥ ᴥ

A MY LOWELL (1874–1925) grew up in a world that may
well have appeared to her as guided by her family in all
the important things. It was common enough in the Boston of
her day and neighborhood for relatives to be wealthy, and
even socially prominent, but the Lowells seemed to have
taken over the arts and sciences as well. If her father's tex-
tile fortune came from the eponymous mill town of Lowell,
her mother's came from similarly eponymous Lawrence.
Amy's brother Lawrence became president of Harvard and
her brother Percival, the astronomer, is purported to have discovered canals on Mars. James Russell Lowell, the poet-
diplomat, was a cousin, as were Guy, the future architect, and
William Lawrence, soon to be bishop of Massachusetts. That
the family tradition has continued to our own day is amply
evidenced in the poetry of Robert.

Of course, any genetic student knows that no important
deductions can be made about families by limiting one's
observations to those descendants who bear a particular sur-
name, but such observations can be important to the bearers
of that name. Amy Lowell knew from infancy that she was a
person to be reckoned with. As her next oldest sibling was

twelve and her parents were middle-aged (and her mother already ailing) when she was born, she had an early training in self-reliance, and her plainness and stoutness taught her at a tender age that life, aside from wealth and social position (which she always took for granted), was not going to heap its bounties into her lap. An unhappily terminated early engagement reinforced her sense of imposed independence, and when at twenty-six she found herself an orphan, she took over the big family estate in Brookline (her siblings were long established in their own homes) and settled down to the busy life of a Boston lady of means, organizing charitable events, sitting on boards of civic institutions, travelling and entertaining.

The obesity that loomed so constantly in her public image may have strengthened her character, as polio did that of Franklin Roosevelt. But it also caused her terrible hernia troubles, necessitated drastic operations and contributed to her early demise. Ezra Pound referred to her cruelly as the "hippopoetess," and she herself once ruefully described her own body as "a disease." Some observers saw in her passionate admiration, expressed in dedicated poems, of the beauty of the actresses Eleanora Duse and Eleanor Robson Belmont evidence of repressed lesbian tendencies, but I see it rather as a longing for the beauty she never had. Indeed, her poetry could be described as a hymn to beauty, and it is fitting that Keats should have been her master poet.

In the ample interstices of her social life she was omnivorously reading literature and its history. She had also started collecting first editions and manuscripts, and in 1905 she made her first important purchase of Keatsiana. But curiously enough, she wrote hardly at all. It was not until she saw Duse in the d'Annunzio plays in Boston in 1902 that she had something like an apocalyptic experience. She wrote:

The effect on me was something tremendous. What really happened was that it revealed me to myself, but I hardly knew that at the time. I just knew that I had to express the sensations that Duse's acting gave me, somehow. I knew nothing whatever about the technique of poetry. I had never heard of *vers libre*, I had never analyzed blank verse — I was as ignorant as anyone could be. I sat down and with infinite agitation wrote this poem.

She had found her career and she went to work, but it was eleven more years before she published her first book of poetry, *A Dome of Many-Colored Glass*. It was generally regarded as a weak start, but it was a start, and from then on she published regular volumes of increasingly finer quality until her death, which was followed by several posthumous ones.

But the considerable fame that she achieved as a poet was exceeded by her reputation as a formidable fighter for the acceptance of the "new poetry." Amy Lowell had the pugnacious blood of the old abolitionists, even though the textile-owning Lawrences and Lowells had had some sympathy with the old planters of antebellum days. She fiercely wanted a cause, and she found one in free verse, enchanted to take on the vociferous opposition of the old guard, who rallied around the flag of Ella Wheeler Wilcox and shouted for regular rhymes and sugar-coated sentimentality. She travelled over the country giving lectures and readings, poured her money into needy poetry periodicals and the pockets of needy "advanced" poets, gave newspaper interviews and made her great house in Brookline the social capital of the movement. Her stout, redoubtable figure, cigar in mouth, was the subject of cartoons from coast to coast.

She added the new imagist school to her list of causes. She proclaimed herself one, a poet who (1) used the language of common speech and always the exact word, (2) created new rhythms, (3) insisted on absolute freedom of subject, (4) presented an image and (5) produced poetry that was hard and clear.

It was never entirely clear just what a true imagist was, or even whether Miss Lowell was one. Pound, again the wag, called her an "Amygist," but the tussle was exhilarating.

And the public loved the details of her schedule. The daily, or rather nightly routine at Brookline, when she was not away lecturing or attending poetry conferences, was certainly un-Bostonian. Mrs. Ada Russell, the companion and housekeeper who had given up a stage career to manage Miss Lowell's life, oversaw the running of the house and grounds and arranged the lively dinner parties that supplied the exchange of ideas on which the poetess depended. The guests were seated at table by eight o'clock; Miss Lowell was always a bit late. After the meal the party adjourned to the library, where towels were supplied to protect their clothing from the salivary affections of seven large sheep dogs. Nobody abandoned the brisk discussion before midnight, when the party broke up, and Miss Lowell, settled in a deep leather armchair before the fire, wrote until dawn or later, leaving on the hall table the sheets for her secretary to type in the morning and climbing to her childhood bedroom on the third floor to sleep into the afternoon.

On her constant travels she was accompanied by Mrs. Russell and one or sometimes two maids. At hotels she required a suite of five rooms: a bedroom with a vacant room on either side, a sitting room and a room for Mrs. Russell, besides accommodation for the maids. All electric clocks had to be stopped and all mirrors covered, and Miss Lowell's double bed had to be furnished with sixteen pillows.

Was the war for the new poetry worth it? Probably not.

Readers would have turned to free verse without Amy Lowell's crusade. But the conflict generated some lively and provocative discussions and may have stimulated creative activity, and it certainly gave a lot of people considerable mental exercise and pleasure. If the same energy had been invested in a needier cause, say in the sadly neglected civil rights of the era, a greater social good might have been effected, but it is ungracious to downgrade benevolent deeds of the past because they could have been more benevolent. Let us be glad when people care enough about any good cause to fight for it.

More important is the question of how much the issues at stake in the poetry war affected Miss Lowell's own verse. How much did she herself profit from the wider horizons now available to her art?

She certainly achieved some dazzling effects in the exotic and colorful settings of her poems. An expert in prosody, she experimented with every known form of versification, including what she called "polyphonic prose," a kind of orchestral form, but her relentless emphasis on the individual vivid image was, at least in my opinion, at the ultimate expense of the thought content of her verse. In "The Bronze Horses," for example, a reader may be initially charmed by this description of a Roman patrician lady of the era of Titus in her bath:

Her breasts round hollows for themselves in the sky-green water, her fingers sift the pale water and drop it from her as a lark drops notes backwards into the sky. The lady lies against the lipping water, supine and indolent, a pomegranate, a passion flower, a silver-flamed lily, lapped, slapped, lulled by the ripples which stir under her faintly moving hands.

But when the reader comes to the quoted remarks of the Roman spectators at the games, he might be hearing the dialogue of a Hollywood script writer for such a spectacle as *Quo Vadis* or *The Sign of the Cross*: "It's been abominably monotonous lately. Why, there's not enough blood spilled in the games last week to give me the least appetite."

Or this, in relation to a slave market: "I had rather a fancy for a Jewess. I'll get her, by Bacchus, if I have to mortgage my farm."

After these, when one returns to the lady in her bath one can think only of Claudette Colbert as the Empress Poppaea, lolling in a pool of milk.

F. Cudworth Flint has put the problem of Lowell's imagery succinctly and well:

> Miss Lowell's command of cadence and color, and her ability to sustain animation, are amazing. But to be amazed so prolongedly results at last in exhausted stupefaction. The experience is akin to traversing interminable corridors adorned with tapestries whose patterns are intricate, insistent, and, finally, incapacitating.

What of her many volumes will survive? I think that "Patterns" and "Lilacs," old favorites and deservedly so, will always find a niche in anthologies of American verse. And some of the others, oddly enough the ones that owe least to her passion for color and exoticism, those rare poems of hers which are based on a deep personal grief or emotion, may keep her name alive. I offer two quotations.

The first is from "On Looking at a Copy of Alice Meynell's Poems, Given me, Years ago, by a Friend." The friend, at least so it seems to me, was a man whom she loved but who failed to return her love and wished to be kind.

And I remember how they rang,
These words, like bronze cathedral bells
Down ancient lawns, or citadels
Thundering with gongs where choirs sang.

Silent the sea, the earth, the sky,
And in my heart a silent weeping.
Who has not sown can know no reaping!
Bitter conclusion and no lie.

O heart that sorrows, heart that bleeds,
Heart that was never mine, your words
Were like the pecking Autumn birds
Stealing away my garnered seeds.

The second is from "A Communication," a supposed letter addressed to a different sort of man, one who has deserted her.

Because I wished to believe,
I saw in your Byronic gesture of woe,
Not what it purported to be, certainly,
But something not too different.
You cast a larger shadow than yourself, that I realized,
But even I, who should have known better,
Believed it was your shadow.
I crave your pardon for my blunder.
The mask was well assumed.
I should have been critical enough to understand it was
    an artistic production.

I congratulate you on the verisimilitude of it.
But I shall not be fooled again, be sure of that.
In future I shall see you as you are:

A plaster figure of a man that's grown a little dusty.
We all have knick-knacks round which once meant
    something.
It is rather a wrench to take them from their niches,
But life goes on imperious, and bric-a-brac accumulates.

At the time of her death many considered that her massive two-volume life of Keats, just published, would be her most lasting contribution to letters. Time has not borne this out. Keats has had some excellent recent biographers, in particular Aileen Ward and Robert Gittings, whose work has superseded Lowell's. The massive research in which she engaged has lightened the work of her successors, but few readers today would care to revisit her laborious though meticulous details when they can avail themselves of the more compressed conclusions of later students.

But there is a greater objection to Miss Lowell's *Keats.* Her devotion to her subject is too steamy, too abject. She is like a doting mother or a fond maiden aunt. Her "John" can do no wrong, and she seeks to rebut evidence of his syphilis or what he himself called his "venery." She has his sad early end constantly in view, and she indulges in such interjections as "Poor boy! He had only four years and a fraction" to live. On occasion she makes no secret of her blind partiality:

> I have omitted a reference to a young man named Newmarch, who, Stephens insists, ridiculed Keats's poetry and made broad fun of his brothers for their admiration of it. The reason for my omission is that I do not believe in the existence of Newmarch. Stephens says that "he came often," having formerly been intimate with Keats. But Keats was the last man in the world to permit anyone who was rude to his brothers to come even once again.

If one can discount the author's strong bias — and Keats's own charm of character makes this almost possible — the fine vigorous prose of the book and Miss Lowell's narrative flair and critical acumen about the poems discussed will carry one through. She is particularly effective in her vivid descriptions of Keats's numerous friends, loyal and disloyal. But the particular charm of the work is in the relationship of the author and the subject and their joint submission to the muse of poetry. It is not so much a biography as a kind of missal to the art of verse.

I. Compton-Burnett

۶ ۶ ۶

THE LITERARY LIFE OF Ivy Compton-Burnett (1884– 1969) was late in developing. Although she published her first novel, *Dolores*, at her own expense at the age of only twenty-seven, she tried to buy in all the copies, and her second, *Pastors and Masters*, had to wait another fourteen years to appear. Thereafter, however, she published novels almost bi-annually until her death. The writing of fiction became the staple of her life and certainly the source of her keenest pleasure. She neither married nor had love affairs; "I'm neuter," she used to say. Certainly the grim little old lady in the famous Cecil Beaton photograph, with the opaquely staring eyes, the thin tight lips, the clasped hands and the hair bound with a thin fillet across the brow, is not suggestive of pleasures other than cerebral.

Yet she was not always so. As a young woman she had been almost pretty and even inclined to giggles and high spirits. She was the daughter of a famous and prosperous homeopathic doctor who raised the many children of his two marriages in a large house in Hove, near Brighton. Nothing was put in the way of any career Ivy should choose for herself; she went to Holloway College and made many friends, especially among the brilliant group of her adored younger brother, Noel, and even, as noted, published a novel. But the death of her mother in 1911 (the doctor had died a decade earlier) brought about a sudden and unfortunate change in her life.

Ivy deemed it her duty and destiny to take over the management of the real properties in which her father had invested his considerable savings and run the household for her four younger sisters. But she did this with a grimness and sobriety quite out of keeping with her age. As one observer put it: "Those were years in which Ivy wasn't master of herself — something was mastering her, and it wasn't the best part of her." She became an intolerant domestic tyrant, like many of the villains of her later fiction. Her excellent biographer, Hilary Spurling, describes her at this time:

> When her sisters foregathered in the music room, she sat alone downstairs in her father's study. She disapproved of their friends, mistrusted their ambitions, seldom joined in their activities, often scarcely saw them except at meals for weeks on end. When the others went bathing and practised fancy strokes or dived off the pier, Ivy would swim out at a steady breast stroke so far that her family used to worry sometimes if she would ever come back.

And probably hoped at times that she wouldn't. Revolt was inevitable. All four sisters at last moved to London and set up their own establishment, where Ivy was not welcome; she was left to get her own flat when she followed them. Soon the Great War engulfed them all. In 1916 Noel, the light of Ivy's life, was killed in the Battle of the Somme, where Haig sacrificed a quarter of a million men to gain a few miles of mud and trenches. None of it made any sense to Ivy; she despised the war. Then, in 1917, her two youngest sisters committed suicide; both had been on drugs. How bad she felt about this we do not know, but she must have had moments of feeling that she could have been more sympathetic with them. Finally, Ivy suffered a severe nervous breakdown and almost died in the flu epidemic.

In *Dolores*, the strangely inept little novel whose publication she all her life regretted, the heroine sacrifices her own happiness at every turn to what she deems the best interests of her family and friends, and she ends up, not only wretched herself, but without having furthered the good fortune of any of the objects of her bounty. It is hard to tell what point the author is trying to make; at moments one cannot but wonder if the tale is not a kind of parody of a sober George Eliot theme. In any event, she turned violently against the whole concept of self-sacrifice. This dialogue from *Mother and Son* sufficiently expresses her ultimate point of view:

"I never know why self-sacrifice is noble," said Miss Burke.

"Why is it better to sacrifice oneself than someone else?"

"It is no better," said Hester, "and it is not really held to be."

"It does not seem that we ought to matter ourselves as much as other people," said Emma. "But I have never met a case of self-sacrifice."

"It would be trying to be the object of it," said Hester.

"That would be the best thing to be," said Miss Burke. "There would be some compensation."

"Sacrifice should be anonymous, or it does not deserve the name."

"But then it would not be made," said Emma. "It would really deserve it."

Ivy was now determined to live for herself. Only an intelligent self-interest should guide one in living with one's fellow men — for their good as well as one's own. She was fortunate right after the war to find a friend with whom she could share a home, an arrangement that lasted until Margaret Jourdain's death, in 1950. The two women could not have been more different; it was the attraction of opposites. Jourdain was a famous decorator, a national authority on furniture, paneling, plaster carving, embroidery and lace; she was a vivacious and witty hostess with a sparkling circle of sophisticated friends. Inevitably, in the early years of their joint household and before Ivy gained fame as a writer, the latter was known, as one friend put it, as the "rather stout middle-class woman who poured out cups of tea for all the young men who came to see Margaret." But they began to gather around Ivy and collect her trenchant comments when literary London gradually became aware that a new star had swum into its ken.

Between 1925 and 1963 Ivy published eighteen novels. A posthumous one, *The Last and First,* followed in 1971. Nathalie Sarraute has proclaimed her one of the most important novelists of the century and the leader in England of the *nouveau roman*. Joyce Carol Oates, on the other hand, finds that her vogue has largely passed and has criticized her "use of puppet characters in sketchily realized settings" as suggesting an imaginative deficiency.

I come down on Sarraute's side. I suggest that what Ivy was really doing, though she was never in the least articulate about it, was jettisoning the whole format of the novel as it had hitherto existed: the drama, the plot, the endlessly analyzed characters, the full descriptive passages. She may have agreed with Sarraute's thesis in *L'Ère du Soupçon* that readers had begun to suspect that the whole business of fiction was bogus, that the author was hiding behind a character and peeking out at them, that he was trying to *be* the character when all the while it was just the author in a silly hat. And this game of the authors, once embarked upon, encouraged them to let their imaginations run wild and attribute all kinds of heroics and deviltries to their characters, to romanticize them, to romanticize mankind, to puff up his passions and adventures, his aspirations and his downfalls, to make the whole business of living seem a much more adventurous and thrilling experience than it could possibly be except to a handful of gifted souls.

Ivy and Sarraute, in short, agreed with Thoreau that most men lead lives of quiet desperation. To show this, to show man at his most characteristic moments, Ivy didn't want eras of revolution or violent change, which distort his normal feelings and reactions; she saw that she could best use the peaceful, quiet countryside of the English upper middle class in the setting sun of the empire, leaving the thunder of war to far-off colonies, where unmanageable natives had to be disciplined for impudence by armies of younger sons. Only when men and women had leisure, preferably too much leisure, when their principal social activity lay in making calls and talking, would they most effectively demonstrate their own natures and their need to dominate others or to resist that domination. How could one see them better than in their own words? How did they differ from animals except in their minds, and how could they show their minds but in their words? "Words are all we have," one of Ivy's characters asserts, to which another replies: "They are used as if they had some power. And how little they have!" But that little was enough for Ivy to delineate the endless friction of human relations, the constant attack and the inevitable retaliations, like bugs, enlarged in a nature movie, ceaselessly eating each other and being eaten.

But to return to Joyce Carol Oates's point. Why are Ivy's characters described in such drab, flat detail, their eyes being given primary colors and their features exact dimensions, their faces banal expressions of reaction and their clothes common styles? Why are Ivy's plots filled with all the hack devices of Victorian popular fiction: forged documents, destroyed wills, persons deemed dead suddenly reappearing, illegitimate births, adulteries, larcenies and even murder?

I think the descriptions of the characters are like the cast in a playbill, there purely for purposes of identification. Ivy's novels are close to the theatre; they are made up largely, sometimes almost entirely, of dialogue. She would really, I believe, have been happy to have written them as plays, but the play form was too compact for her purposes. She had to inform us, anyway, what each character looked like, so that we could tell them apart — they were not, after all, before us as on a stage.

But the clumsiness of the melodrama in Ivy's plots is harder to explain. Are we ready for Josephine Napier's sudden murder of her daughter-in-law in *More Women than Men* or for its being witnessed by a fellow teacher who fails to denounce it? Can we really believe that Hereward Egerton in *A God and His Gifts* would seduce his son's fiancée, adopt the resulting bastard and then persuade his son to marry the girl? Would the supposedly drowned Ellen Mowbray in *A Father and His Fate* really have played Enoch Arden? It is, of course, possible that Ivy did not regard these twists of plot as unrealistic; she always maintained that the events she described occurred more frequently in life than people generally imagined. But I suspect that she used these events as ways of turning her dialogues to deeper themes and varying their tones; she was like a director who changes his sets without lowering the curtain; he must prove that he is not trying to fool you into thinking that you are not in a theatre watching actors. "Here is what I am doing! I am being perfectly honest with you at all times!" That for him may be the supreme art.

The melodrama also relieves the long dialogues of what without them might become monotony. The reader is ready for some action, and the artificial though arresting quality of the talk prepares him for a certain quaintness in the events. One might even say that the quaintness offers a kind of semi-comic parody of the plot devices of romantic literature. It is also in keeping with Ivy's belief that the passions pass as lightly over most folk as do lesser emotions. If Josephine Napier's fierce possessiveness over her adoptive son is strong enough to induce her in a reckless moment to kill his bride, it is not strong enough to keep her from preferring another man to him a month later, nor will that other man's twenty-year homosexual liaison with one old enough to be his father keep him from a happy and romantic marriage with a beautiful young woman.

The human drama in Ivy's novels is apt to act itself out in the struggle between one or more strong-minded elderly ego-tists to dominate a family group and the resistance, often suc-cessful, of a larger number of formally subservient but actively critical younger members. The would-be leader expresses himself or herself in dogmatic, self-laudatory assertions of devotion to duty while the audience cuts down the speaker in murmured witticisms among one another which are usually overheard. It is comedy, but as Adrian observes in *Mother and Son*, comedy is a wicked way of looking at tragedy when it is not our own.

Ivy's two constant *motifs* of fatuous self-esteem and devas-tating exposure following each other as in a fugue, strophe and antistrophe, are well illustrated by this interchange between a married couple in *A God and His Gifts* as they discuss their economic plight:

"Ah, no one is the worse for our downfall. That must be our stay. Without it we were poor indeed."

"It sounds as if we should be poor with it. And some people must be the worse, if you mean we are in debt."

"We must not bring faint hearts to the stress of life. We must face our indebtedness, shoulder the burden and carry it with us. We will not bend beneath it, heavy though it be. Is not that our own victory?"

"Yes, it is. We can be sure it would not be anyone else's."

"Ah, the humble part is the hard one. Gratitude is the rare thing to give. In a sense it is a gift. If we can give it, nothing is beyond us. To render it is the way to be unvanquished by it."

"It must be difficult to be vanquished," said Joanna. "I hardly see how anyone could be."

Ivy believed above all else in seeing the world without illusion. She wanted to be in absolute charge of her own life. If each individual would only look after himself, was her credo, the world might make some sense. Intelligent self-interest could be a moral code. When asked on her eightieth birthday what she had learned in a long life, she replied, after some thought, "That people are morally the same but intellectually different." As her friends dropped off, one by one, she would ask about the end of each and then nod, with some remark such as "Of a stroke? Good, good. And she had her maid to the last? Good."

ELINOR WYLIE

⁂

E LINOR WYLIE (1884–1928) as a young bride at a Washington party attempted to hold a lighted match until it
burned out, shifting the end held, to see if somebody loved
her. She succeeded in burning a piece out of her nail. Horace
Wylie, who became her lover and second husband, watched
the experiment and later prescribed the reading of Jane
Welsh Carlyle's letters to calm her nerves.

Much of her early life can be seen in the incident: her
romanticism, her daring, her defiance — even perhaps her
incapacity for lasting love.

She was born to an affluent Philadelphia family, but raised
in Washington, where her father, Henry Hoyt, served as
Theodore Roosevelt's solicitor general. Bright and beautiful,
but not marked by any early manifestation of literary genius,
she married at the age of twenty the handsome but unre-
markable son of an admiral, Philip Hichborn, and embarked
on the routine social round of the younger set in the nation's
capital. But it soon became evident that this was not going to
satisfy her. She fell in love with an older married man, a
lawyer of some means and literary tastes, Horace Wylie, and
eloped with him to England, deserting her infant son.

The scandal that this aroused seems excessive in retrospect, even for 1910. The couple were completely ostracized at home, and even apparently abroad, for they lived obscurely in an English village under an assumed name. Katherine Wylie refused for six years to give her husband a divorce or to allow him to see his children, and she even used her influence in Washington after he returned to keep him from getting appointments. The fact that Philip Hichborn committed suicide and that Elinor had left her son may have exacerbated the feeling against her, but why she and Horace could not have found a more tolerant society in certain circles of Paris or even London is a mystery.

At any rate in 1916 Katherine Wylie at last agreed to a divorce, and Horace and Elinor were able to marry and reconstitute their lives in New York. There, in the 1920s, Elinor found her true bailiwick. Her striking looks, her hauteur, her wit, made her a centre of attention at Greenwich Village gatherings of writers and artists, where she must have appeared as much more the great lady than the scarlet woman. She had begun to publish her striking verses, and in 1923 she succeeded Edmund Wilson as literary editor of *Vanity Fair* in the heyday of Frank Crowninshield, who said of her, "She liked to pretend that she was Bohemian, but the sham was at all times apparent."

At parties she always had a group of literary men around her. As Stanley Olson put it:

> First they thought they were protecting her, then they learned she needed no protection. Yet they still formed a cohort around her. They were vulnerable to her femininity; they were mesmerized by her talent; and they were flattered by her acquaintance. She never failed to overlook the value of their relationships while deliberately failing to make them more important. Elinor was never an intimate

of any group . . . Her fascination lay in her complexity. The closer people got, the more shadowy she became, and yet from a distance observers thought they understood her. She was classified as vain, egocentric and temperamental, and she was all of these, but they were little more than an insulation, a veneer, that completely hid anything underneath.

Other observers were less favorable. Thomas Wolfe found her "a horrible woman" and managed to insult her. Virginia Woolf found her "a hatchet-minded, cadaverous, acid-voiced, bareboned, spavined, patriotic, nasal, thick-legged American [who] proclaimed unimpeachable truths and discussed our sales; hers are three times greater than mine."

Poor old Horace Wylie couldn't keep up with her new life and was dropped in favor of her third husband, the poet and critic William Rose Benét. Yet Elinor's retort to Tallulah Bankhead's query "You've had lots of lovers, haven't you?" may well have been true: "I've had no lovers at all, Tallulah — that's why I had three husbands. When I've fallen in love, I have married."

And it was like her when, with a sense of impending death (she had always suffered from high blood pressure), in 1927 she wrote to Horace Wylie: "I am going to admit that I wish with all my heart I had never left you . . . do not think I am divorcing Bill . . . He is the best boy imaginable . . . But I loved you first, I loved you more, I loved him afterwards, but now that I love you both, I love you best."

Or might she have said: I love you neither? Rebecca West remarked that Elinor always wanted people she could not count on getting.

Her real life had to be in literature. She was very proud of her novels, and *Jennifer Lorn* had a considerable critical and popular success, but her fiction is little read today. Her style is polished and lacquered to the intentionally absurd, and her characters brightly painted dolls. She creates some vivid pictures, with the brightest colors, and amuses with occasional wit, but the overall effect is one of great tedium. The hero of *The Venetian Glass Nephew* is just that; he is made of glass. Such a character can sustain one's interest in only the very shortest sketch — or can amuse children in an Oz story. Wylie was upset when a friend found her working with an encyclopedia; she feared that the observer might think she had got all her historical details from such "boning up." The observer may well have been correct.

As Wylie began to put her life together in the 1920s it was in poetry that she found her strength and mainstay. The chaos of her wrecked tribal life and the threatened chaos of the postwar world seemed to merge to offer her — as they offered to other disoriented souls — the intoxicating prospect of liberty from the claustrophobia of upper-middle-class morals and the bleakness of social interdict. But like so many other pioneers of that new and dangerous frontier, like Millay and Fitzgerald and Wilson and even Hemingway, she clung fiercely to one discipline, to one faith: her passion for the exact right word, the hard glittering beauty of the chiseled, jeweled phrase.

A young poet of the time, who unfortunately gave up her art at an early date, a debutante of the era who was sometimes published in *Vanity Fair*, Helen Choate, well expressed this passion in a poem called "Archery":

Yet think how words too many tongues have dulled,
Words cruel that have lost the power to harrow,
And tender words, too worn for seeming sweet,

And phrases petty usage has made narrow,
May by a poet be set in a new design
And sharpened to the pattern of an arrow.

And think of this: the ringed and circled target —
The target towards which such arrows go —
And how a dart thus fashioned by a poet,
Sent swift and flying from a poet's bow,
May strike and quiver at its center circle,
And reach the very heart of beauty so.

Wylie turned away from the blown richness of a lush summer as she turned from the blowsy complacence of Victorian domesticity. The Puritan core in her, which is almost impossible for any experience to extract, enabled her to draw a strange ecstasy from punishment, as Hester Prynne did in *The Scarlet Letter.*

Down to the Puritan marrow of my bones
There's something in this richness that I hate.
I love the look, austere, immaculate,
Of landscapes drawn in pearly monotones.
There's something in my very blood that owns
Bare hills, cold silver, on a sky of slate,
A thread of water, churned to milky spate
Streaming through slanted pastures fenced with stones.

I love those skies, thin blue or snowy gray,
Those fields, sparse-planted, rendering meager sheaves;
That spring, briefer than apple-blossom's breath,
Summer, so much too beautiful to stay,
Swift autumn, like a bonfire of leaves,
And sleepy winter, like the sleep of death.

To avoid the "reeking herd," the "huddled warmth of crowds," one might emulate the lone eagle staring into the sun, or if that were beyond the leaping capacity of one's senses, one should be as the "velvet mole," hiding underground with the roots of trees and disembodied bones. For the world is full of hate, and if one has to live in it, the best one can hope is to be like the figure in "A Proud Lady":

> What has it done, this world,
> With hard fingertips,
> But sweetly chiseled and curled
> Your inscrutable lips?

In her need for the simple beauties of nature she had little enough use for men — and even less for God, who like the crowd seemed to be always intruding on her privacy.

> He turned His burning eyes on me
> From smoke above a mountain shelf;
> I did not want his company
> Who wanted no one but myself.

> I whistled shrill, I whistled keen;
> The birds were servant to my nod.
> They wove their wings into a screen
> Between my lovely ground and God.

Into my favorite of all her poems, "Innocent Landscape," she poured the essence of her creed. The "breath of miracle," the creation of the universe, is nothing but confusion. Faith, such as it is, may have come out of the cursing of the fruit after the apple has been bitten, but all is blighted; only the poor landscape itself has had no part in it.

Here is no peace, although the air has fainted,
And footfalls die and are buried in deep grass,
And reverential trees are softly painted
Like saints upon an oriel of glass.

The pattern of the atmosphere is spherical,
A bubble in the silence of the sun,
Blown thinner by the very breath of miracle
Around a core of loud confusion.

Here is no virtue; here is nothing blessèd
Save this foredoomed suspension of the end;
Faith is the blossom, but the fruit is cursèd;
Go hence, for it is useless to pretend.

And man, "egregious egotist," imagines that he alone of
created fauna is sentient!

He asks no questions of the snake,
Nor plumbs the phosphorescent gloom
Where lidless fishes, broad awake,
Swim staring at a nightmare doom.

If there was any survival of the human soul in ultimate
unity with the spirit of the universe, the speck of life it
had once been she expressed in verse reminiscent of Emily
Dickinson's:

Before division of the suns
Take shears to cut a second's thread,
The mind must tick ecstatic once
To prove that it is dead.

And the small soul's dissolving ghost
Must leave a heart-shape in the dust
Before it is inspired and lost
In God: I hope it must.

And she could also be a satirist. She knew how to handle
the heroic couplet of Pope, almost as well as T. S. Eliot did in
the passages of "The Waste Land" that Ezra Pound unfortunately (in my view at least) induced him to cut.

She gives a false impression that she's pretty
Because she has a soft, deceptive skin
Saved from her childhood; yet it seems a pity
That she should be as vain of this as sin:
Her mind might bloom, she might reform the world
In those lost hours while her hair is curled.

I like to take my leave of this charming poet with a stanza
from "A Tear for Cressid," her humorous apologia for her
own disordered love life.

Let the pure and noble go hand in hand
To the service of God addressed;
But ye whose hearts are as shifting sand
Speak but a word for Cressid:
Let bridal pairs in their arrased halls
Lie in honor and pride embraced:
But all ye fond lovers who ever were false
Come drink to the health of Cressid.

HAROLD NICOLSON

※ ※ ※

Pᴇʀᴄʏ Lᴜʙʙᴏᴄᴋ said of Edith Wharton that her books had to be written on the "bare margin of such a populous and ornamental existence." His comment arouses the speculation of whether her art would have been improved by greater concentration. Might a more deeply conceived *House of Mirth* have ranked with *Anna Karenina*? Of course we can never know, but I tend to believe that it was necessary for Edith Wharton to live more or less actively in the milieu that formed the setting for her major novels, and that when she lost touch with New York society in her later expatriate years the quality of her fiction notably declined. Henry James in his younger days in France and England was an intensely social being (he dined out 140 times in one London winter), but after he had amassed his own little capital of observations and *données*, he was able to settle down more quietly and comfortably in Rye. I doubt that anyone has ever suggested that Shakespeare's acting and theatrical management or T. S. Eliot's banking or Conrad's marine life detracted from their writing, though I am sure that both Racine and Gerard Manley Hopkins would have produced more and perhaps even greater poetry without the erosion of their time and energy in religious devotion. What outside activities hinder or aid an artist is difficult to assess.

A prime example of a busy and fruitful life in the "great world" that was entirely compatible with the quantity (thirty-five volumes) and high quality of his literary output was that of Harold Nicolson (1886–1968). I do not believe that he would have written any better had he given up his public life and devoted himself (as his wife always wished him to) exclusively to letters. He was one of those happy souls who realized to the fullest all of his potentials. Not by any means the greatest of diplomats or parliamentarians, and not the finest of English biographers or historians, he nonetheless made his distinctive and distinguished mark in each field of his endeavors.

He was born into the diplomatic service and spent much of his boyhood in his father's (Lord Carnock's) posts in Budapest, Tangier, Constantinople and Saint Petersburg, but he attended public school in England and Balliol College in Oxford. From 1909 to 1929 he served in the Foreign Office with appointments to Madrid, Istanbul, Teheran and Berlin. He then switched to journalism, working as a columnist for Lord Beaverbrook on the *Evening Standard*; but not finding this to his taste, he joined the dwindling ranks of Ramsay Mac-Donald's National Labour Party and was elected to Parliament for Leicestershire with Conservative Party backing. He remained in the House of Commons until 1945, leaving it, as his good friend Winston Churchill put it, a "sadder place," after which he devoted the major part of his time to writing. He was married to the novelist Vita Sackville-West, and they lived not far from her beloved family seat, Knole, in picturesque Sissinghurst Castle, where they developed and tended one of the most beautiful gardens in England.

Nicolson's literary works include two novels, biographies of

Tennyson, Byron, Sainte-Beuve, Swinburne, Dwight Morrow, George Curzon and George V, and of his uncle Lord Dufferin and his father Lord Carnock, books on diplomacy, peace-making, royalty and travel, and his one classic, *Some People*, a delightful fusion of fiction and memoir about curious individuals encountered in the course of his academic and diplomatic career. There are also his posthumously published journals, an illuminating record of his era in which just about every person of note in the political, artistic and social worlds of Great Britain makes an appearance. If in all of his work Nicolson paints a colorful picture of the glowing sunset of a great empire from the viewpoint of one of its privileged sons, his canvas is still a fine one.

His life may have been crammed with good things, but he had his share of worries. He was afflicted with a nervous insecurity, a kind of wavering self-doubt, a failure of the competitive spirit which always kept him from obtaining the first position in the worlds of politics and diplomacy. He suffered as a child from strange and irrational panics, and in *Helen's Tower* he suddenly and harshly lashes out at his old governess, Miss Plimsoll, whom he had treated with such humorous kindliness in *Some People*, accusing her of instilling false values in her ward. "It was her beastly infatuation for battleships and commodores and picket boats and little midshipmen attacking Chinese bandits armed only with a dirk which made me feel so constantly unshipshape. The fibres of my own virility, such as they were, were by this process twisted into unnatural shapes."

Is he referring here to the homosexual tastes that he indulged discreetly all his life, with the full consent of his proudly indiscreet lesbian spouse? He seems to have suspected that his relations with young men may have hurt him at the Foreign Office, but the importance of his various assignments abroad offers evidence that the sophisticated British upper classes knew how to look the other way when unconventional addictions were not flaunted. As Nicolson wrote about his life as chargé d'affaires in Teheran, it was "sexless, sinless, simple. Its regularity has about it . . . a certain beauty."

A young diplomat named Patrick, however, could have altered the Iranian sexlessness had he not rejected Nicolson's advances. As the latter wrote, with his usual candor, to Vita, Patrick "with firm but kindly tact made it quite clear to me that he wasn't one of that sort . . . I have already read Patrick the parts of this letter which refer to him. He clearly thinks you must be just as odd as me."

One is sure that Patrick did. The remarkable and ultimately happy adjustment that Harold and Vita made to the seeming contradiction of their sexual urges and their deep mutual love has been amply chronicled by their son Nigel in *Portrait of a Marriage.* Harold always regarded their mutual love as the solider thing; he tended to trivialize his homosexuality. "I think lust is a fine thing, a noble thing. It should never be allowed to get down at heel." He summed it up when he wrote, "I do not like other people's vices." His attitude would not be popular in the gay community today.

Vita was much more serious about her affairs with women. Indeed, she was the stronger character of the two. At first, as I read of the early years of their marriage, when she would leave Harold and their two young sons for months at a time while she was off on passionate trips with the possessive and unscrupulous Violet Trefusis, I was inclined to find her hard and selfish. What about Harold's career in foreign posts where she refused to join him? But ultimately I began to see her point. She had a violent nature and needed to get Violet out of her system. The boys were always well looked after at Knole, and Harold, for all his tearful complaints about how terribly he missed her ("It is simply misery for me, these perpetual departures of yours"), still had his young men. She was desperately bored by politics and diplomacy, and she regarded her husband as much more fitted for a writing career (which in many ways he was), and she had both the money and the willingness to support him. And ultimately at Sissinghurst she was able to provide the perfect life for him.

Her fierce independence of the world, anyway, was attractive. Less so was a certain whimpery quality in her husband, a habit of sentimentality that got him into occasional trouble. He would go into unreasonable fits of panic over Vita's safety, trembling for her life when she was crossing an empty street. His affection for Osbert Mosley kept him from breaking with the New Party until some time after it was perfectly clear that the Fascists had taken it over, and he insisted on continuing his correspondence with Guy Burgess even after that "crapulous traitor" (as Nicolson's excellent biographer, James Lees-Milne, dubs him) had defected to Russia. Nicolson could infuriate his political allies by conceding that his defeat at the polls had been "all for the best," and at the same time could throw a temper tantrum if he arrived as an after-dinner guest at the appointed time and found his host still at the table. Lees-Milne put some of his inconsistencies into an understandable light when he pointed out that, like Benjamin Constant, Nicolson was an aristocrat-bohemian. "Both came to regard politics as their profession, whereas they were primarily literary men. Neither was successful in his presumption, and neither understood that cliché-ridden nonentities often make more effective politicians than men of intellectual brilliance."

But the above are minor faults. It is wise to remember how closely Nicolson's life has been recorded both by himself and others; few of us would escape censure under such a microscope. His books are a better memorial to himself. He loved England, particularly the England of the late Victorian and Edwardian eras; he loved the pageant of Empire, the ceremonies of rank, the Horse Guards, the panoply and the color, the high dedication of the great warriors and ministers of state, and he described it all with a rich pen. This did not mean for a moment that he was unconscious of the cruelty of the slaughter of savages or of the injustices of rank or of the blight of poverty or of the horrors of the Irish potato famine. These things he recorded too, but his imagination was always more stirred by the picturesque and the dramatic.

Take for example his highly critical description of the advantages with which his mother's sister's husband, the Marquis of Dufferin and Ava, a wealthy Irish peer, started life:

On leaving Oxford the road to eminence would be cleared of all subsidiary traffic. Did he hesitate to face the vulgarities of a parliamentary election? An English peerage was at once placed at his disposal. Did he desire to obtain some official position? He had but to call at Downing Street to become a Lord in Waiting. Did foreign travel attract him? There was his schooner, with the chintz and firelight in the cabin and his private physician to care for his health. Was he curious to sample the ardours of warfare? British admirals and French generals violated all regulations to do him honour. Did the Arctic Circle attract him with the silence of its midnight sun? A French frigate, a member of the French Imperial House, was all too glad to take his schooner in tow.

This book, *Helen's Tower*, is to me his finest, for he is able to bring his own memories of his magnificent uncle as ambassador in France and viceroy in India to fill out the picture. Nicolson is always at his best when he can mix his own observations with his research. Lord Dufferin represented all that was finest in the old regime; he had the charm and courtliness and integrity and wisdom of the best kind of landed aristocrat; he was magnificent to look upon and splendid in his great houses, but in the end he was taken in by a slick financial manipulator and ruined. As his nephew put it in a typical Nicolsonian sentence: "The smoke of factory chimneys drifted darkly across the sun-drenched lawns of privilege."

Nicolson undertook some books as jobs, either for the money involved or because he couldn't resist the pressure exerted on him. An example of the latter was his life of King George V. He produced a readable biography, with some particularly interesting chapters on the role of the monarch in constitutional crises, but one feels that Buckingham Palace was constantly looking over his shoulder. As he himself put it to a friend, it was difficult to write the life of a man who, had he not been born what he was, would have made an excellent petty officer in the Royal Navy. His life of the American lawyer and banker Dwight Morrow, the partner in J. P. Morgan & Co. who became ambassador to Mexico and father-in-law of Charles Lindbergh, is probably explained by the fee offered. Nicolson did his homework on the financial deals involved, but he had few insights to bring to bear on the world of Wall Street, and America was never his dish of tea. It is a dull book because the subject bored him.

It was inevitably said of Nicolson as a biographer that he emulated Lytton Strachey, and of course he did, as almost every contemporary writer of lives felt bound to do. Strachey had revolutionized the art. But there is nothing wrong with borrowing a bit of a master's technique. In the description, in his life of Tennyson, of the bard's attraction to Arthur Hallam, Nicolson shows himself a successful Stracheyite:

> And more than all this — more than the mere picture of Thompson's handsome face under the street lamp, more than the sound of Blakeslee's laughter at Brookfield's jokes . . . the way Arthur would burst in, when one was reading Paley, and talk so brilliantly, so fluently, about the derivation of moral sentiments; the way he would let his hand fall gently upon one's shoulder . . . And oh! The way he would take one's arm, on summer's evenings, under the limes!

Nicolson never felt quite at home in Bloomsbury, despite Vita's quasi-romantic involvement with Virginia Woolf. And indeed Bloomsbury never really took him in. They probably suspected that he could never wholly rid himself of the idea that a bohemian was a bit of a bounder. His problem is well expressed in one of the stories of *Some People*, "Lambert Orme," based on that famous exponent of the decadent style, Ronald Firbank. The narrator is hopelessly put off by Orme's absurd affectations, but has to concede at the end that the man he has crossed off as a fop has become, posthumously — having been killed in the war — a distinguished poet. Nicolson could be ironical about everyone, not excepting himself.

His very British upper-class faith in the public school system is manifested in "J. D. Marstock," another tale of *Some People*:

> I am not one of those who thoroughly disbelieve in British education. I have seen so much of the foreign product that

I have come to feel that our school system, if placed on a wider basis, may yet prove best adapted to our national temperament. It is true, of course, that it standardizes character and suppresses originality; that it sometimes ruthlessly subordinates the musical to the gymnastic. I am not convinced, however, that this is a bad thing . . . The physically gifted enjoy for a short space of years a prominence of which it would be ungracious to deprive them: nor do I think it unfitting that during the same period the intellectuals should very frequently and brutally be snubbed. True originality will by such measures merely be pruned to greater florescence; and sham originality will, thank God, be suppressed.

We are not surprised that the author was knighted. Or that Vita, descended from earls and dukes, was embarrassed by such lowly eminence.

MAXWELL ANDERSON

🐾 🐾 🐾

A SINGLE BROADWAY SEASON, that of 1936–1937, witnessed the opening of three new plays by Maxwell Anderson (1888–1957): "The Wingless Victory," "The Masque of
Kings" and "High Tor." Has any living playwright enjoyed
such a success in New York before or since? We may say of
Anderson that he had his triumphs when it was best to have
them: in his own lifetime. His many dramas were turned into
gold both on Broadway and in the movies made of them.
There was little hint, even at the end, of what a dip his reputation would posthumously take.

His family had been poor farmers in western Pennsylvan-
ia until his father, Lincoln Anderson, chose, without having attended any divinity school, to set himself up as a
Baptist preacher of Bible-thumping Fundamentalist beliefs,
and moved his large family to different parishes in Ohio and
Iowa, settling at last in Jamestown, North Dakota. Maxwell,
an early reader and writer of poetry, managed, with many
side jobs, to graduate from the state university in Great Forks
and, after two years of teaching English in high school, to
obtain his master's degree at Leland Stanford. Thereafter he
had a checkered teaching career in schools and colleges be-

cause of his pacifist and socialist views, highly unpopular in a nation soon to be embroiled in World War I. He had reacted strongly against his father's emphatic religiosity, but he had married young (the first of his three wives), and he had a family to support.

Then his career took a strange, a seemingly miraculous turn for the better, when he was invited to come to New York to write for *The New Republic* on the basis, so far as one can tell, of a single poem exulting in the fall of the old European royal dynasties. In six months' time he had moved on to *The Globe* and thence to *The World*, where he wrote editorials and, more importantly, became a friend of Laurence Stallings, the book review editor, a wounded war veteran who yearned to write a play exposing the horrors of Armageddon. Stallings had no skill as a playwright but he had all the needed passion and memories, and Anderson quickly saw what he could do with him. Their collaboration resulted in "What Price Glory?," the big stage hit of 1924. Anderson, though possessed of no savings and burdened with a wife and three small children to support, did not hesitate to rely on this single success in a risky profession to cut his ties with journalism and embark on the career of a full-time playwright. It was a choice he would never have to regret.

He was not only prolific; he proved that he could turn his pen to almost any subject, from the trenches in Flanders to the death of Socrates ("Barefoot in Athens") to murder perpetrated by a malevolent child ("The Bad Seed") to a comedy of modern marital relations ("Saturday's Children"). But his great literary ambition was to revive poetic drama, and as this aim encompassed his most memorable successes — the historical Tudor plays and the Sacco-Vanzetti–based tragedy "Winterset" — it is to these that this essay is addressed.

Anderson stated his faith in the great role played by the theatre in the larger drama of civilization in strong terms which suggest that not all of the paternal religious dynamism had been lost on him:

> The theater is a religious institution devoted entirely to the exaltation of the spirit of man . . . It is a church without a creed, but there is no doubt in my mind that our theater, instead of being, as the evangelical ministers used to believe, the gateway to hell, is as much a worship as the theater of the Greeks . . . The plays that please most and run longest in these dusty alleys are representative of human loyalty, courage, love that purges the soul, grief that ennobles.

That was in 1941. He returned to these thoughts in 1945:

> For the first time in our history the majority of thinking people have come up against a crippling lack of faith. There is no faith, political, religious, social or personal, that remains unshaken nowadays . . . Now a good play cannot be written except out of conviction — for or against — and when conviction wobbles, the theater wobbles . . . The era of good playwrighting is an era of confidence — usually, in retrospect, mistaken — confidence that runs through playwrights, audiences, actors and the whole structure of society.

Anderson tended to see history in simplistic terms: as the struggle of the free soul against tyranny. Like Lord Acton, he believed that absolute power corrupts absolutely. His purpose was a long way from that of Henry Adams, who claimed that he had written a dozen volumes of American history for no other purpose than to satisfy himself whether, by the severest process of stating, with the least possible comment, such facts as seemed sure, in such order as seemed rigorously consequent, he could fix for a familiar moment a necessary sequence of human movement. Anderson, on the contrary, held that the artistic interpreter of events was superior to the mere chronicler. He did not hesitate, for example, to depict Elizabeth I in "Elizabeth the Queen" as a wise, great-minded and essentially benevolent sovereign, and the same woman as a subtly scheming malevolent fiend in "Mary of Scotland."

But, of course, we need not judge Anderson as a historian. He is always primarily a dramatist, verging at times on the melodramatist, and his history plays are patchworks of exciting and eminently actable scenes. "Mary of Scotland" encompasses too many events and covers too much time to constitute an effective dramatic unity, but it was a wonderful vehicle for Helen Hayes, who made it peculiarly her own. "Elizabeth the Queen," more tightly wound around the single episode of Essex's abortive rebellion, which generates the tragedy, is the most successful of all Anderson's plays and was perhaps the greatest triumph of the Lunts. Anderson was always singularly fortunate in his casts.

Now, however, we come to the poetry. Anderson had this to say on the subject:

It is incumbent on the dramatist to be a poet, and incumbent on the poet to be a prophet, dreamer and interpreter of the racial [human race] dream. Men have come a long way from the salt water in the millions of years that lie behind them, and have a long way to go in the millions of

years that lie ahead . . . The theater, more than any other
art, has the power to weld and determine what the race
dreams into what the race will become.

Let us see then how he deals with love, a prime subject of
poetry. Here is a dialogue between the lovers in "Winterset":

MIO:
Why, girl, the transfiguration on the mount
was nothing to your face. It lights from within —
a white chalice holding fire, a flower in flame,
this is your face.

MARIAMNE:
And you shall drink the flame
and never lessen it. And round your head
the aureole shall burn that burns there now,
forever. This I can give you. And so forever
the Freudians are wrong.

Mary Stuart is inspired to a like exaltation by Bothwell:

               There is aching
Fire between us, fire that could take deep hold
And burn down all the marches of the west
And make us great or slay us. Yet it's not to be trusted.
Our minds are not the same.

If only their lots had been humbler!

Would God I'd been born
Deep somewhere in the Highlands, and there met you —
A maid in your path, and you but a Highland bowman
Who needed me.

Turn now from love to jealousy, and we hear the Virgin Queen in her palace at Whitehall, writhing in the bitterness of her arid old-maidhood as she contemplates the love life of her hated rival in Scotland:

> Yes, yes — and it's well sometimes
> To be mad with love, and let the world burn down
> In your own white flame. One reads this in romances —
> Such a love smokes with incense; oh, and it's grateful
> In the nostrils of the gods. Now who would part them
> For considerations of earth? Let them have this love
> This little while — let them bed and board together —
> Drink it deep, be happy — aye.

This is hardly poetry adapted to our time; it is the work of second-rate versifier lost in a Shakespearian fantasy. When Mio in a rage turns on Miriamne, he is a thin echo of Hamlet with Ophelia: "Go, keep yourself chaste for the baker bridegroom — baker and son of a baker — let him get his baker's dozen on you!"

And Judge Gaunt in "Winterset" treats us to a mad scene, a staple of Jacobean tragedy, in which he emulates King Lear on the heath and likens such old men as himself to "whores of daughters, lickers of girls' shoes, contrivers of nastiness in the night, purveyors of perversion, worshipers of possession."

When Anderson is not in the grip of Shakespeare, he makes do with Tennyson. Might not the following be a paraphrase of lines in "Ulysses"?

> This is the glory of earth-born men and women,
> not to cringe, never to yield, but standing,
> take defeat implacable and defiant,
> die unsubmitting.

Anderson was certainly successful in producing at least the illusion of serious drama for audiences in the 1930s. But the only dramatist who would successfully bring poetry back to the stage (if we omit Richard Wilbur's superb translations of Molière and Racine) was T. S. Eliot.

Eliot set his first poetic drama in twelfth-century England — the past was traditionally considered more appropriate for verse than the mundane present — but after the success of "Murder in the Cathedral," his tragedy of the martyrdom of Thomas à Becket, he moved boldly not only into the immediate present but into an aspect of the present utterly remote from the questions of faith which now absorbed him: a fashionable London cocktail party. But if God is everywhere, he must be in a cocktail party, and if there can be murder in a cathedral, there can be salvation in a Belgravian drawing room.

"The Cocktail Party" delivers the Christian evangel in a striking combination of sparkling wit and deep theological reflection. The mysterious, uninvited guest at the party of Edward and Lavinia Chamberlayne, Sir Henry Harcourt-Reilly, is a psychiatrist who is also a kind of apostle, with a mission to save souls. But he sends his patients in very different directions. For the Chamberlaynes, salvation will lie in patching up their cracked marriage and continuing their daily lives and daily duties, he learning to cope with his inability to love and she with her unlovability. A part of the good life prescribed to them may even consist in giving and attending cocktail parties. But a very distant destiny awaits Celia Coplestone. She will become a missionary and die crucified by savages on an anthill. And her decision and that of the Chamberlaynes will be equally acceptable to God.

The play with its beautiful message had to be conceived and executed in poetry. No other medium could have reconciled the jarring notes of witty superficiality and dedication to the better life. Julia Shuttlethwaite, who is at once an addled but charming old scatterbrain and a secret agent of the apostle-psychiatrist, has to talk in different ways. On one hand she will chatter along like this:

Well, my dears, and here I am!
I seem *literally* to have caught you napping!
I know I'm much too early; but the fact is, my dears,
That I have to go on to the Gunnings' party —
And you know what *they* offer in the way of food and drink!
And I've had to miss my tea, and I'm simply ravenous
And dying of thirst. What can Parkinson's do for me?
Oh, yes, I know this is a Parkinson party;
I recognized one of their men at the door —
An old friend of mine, in fact.

But with Harcourt-Reilly she will describe Celia's qualifications for her grim missionary tasks quite differently:

Henry, you simply do not understand innocence.
She will be afraid of nothing; she will never even know
That there is anything there to be afraid of.
She is too humble. She will pass between the scolding hills,
Through the valley of decision, like a child sent on an errand
In eagerness and patience. Yet she must suffer.

And Harcourt-Reilly must be able to burst into ribald song at the cocktail party, and later in his office be grave indeed in explaining to Celia Coplestone her options.

REILLY:
There is another way, if you have the courage.

The first I could describe in familiar terms
Because you have seen it, as we all have seen it,
Illustrated, more or less, in lives of those about us.
The second is unknown and so requires faith —
The kind of faith that issues from despair.
The destination cannot be described;
You will know very little until you get there;
You will journey blind. But the way leads towards possession
Of what you have sought for in the wrong place.

CELIA:
That sounds like what I want. But what is my duty?

REILLY:
Whichever way you choose will prescribe its own duty.

CELIA:
Which way is better?

REILLY:
Neither way is better.
Both ways are necessary. It is also necessary
To make a choice between them.

CELIA:
Then I choose the second.

This is great poetry *and* great drama, both beyond Maxwell
Anderson. The latter's magic was that of a deft craftsman
who couldn't write a bad scene or a great play.

S. N. Behrman

❧ ❧ ❧

W HEN SAMUEL N. BEHRMAN (1893–1973) died in his New York City apartment at the age of eighty, his obituary notice recalled that his multitudinous friends in show business, "from Vienna to Malibu," had dubbed him the eighth of the seven lively arts. It further described him as "a short, compact bald man with a kindly disposition, an owlish countenance and a talent for gentle mockery," in short, a character from one of his own parlor comedies.

Yet the high life that he portrayed on the stage had little to do with his early background. He was born the son of a poor Jewish grocer, a student of the Talmud, in Worcester, Massachusetts, as he described in a moving record of his childhood, *The Worcester Account.* But his father was always anxious that his children should be readers, and by the time he managed to send Sam to Clark University for two years and then to Harvard, the youth was already a student of the drama and an eager participant in George Pierce Baker's workshop. He continued his work in the drama at Columbia under Brander Matthews and thereafter supported himself as best he could in journalism and free-lancing until such time as he could get one of the plays he was always writing produced.

He worked for a time in the book review department of

The New York Times, but when assigned to the "Queries and Answers" section, his imagination ran away with him and he began composing witty replies to questions that he himself had sent in. Though these were considerably more amusing than what the regular mail produced, Adolph Ochs, alerted to the trick, was not amused, and Behrman was fired. In 1927, however, his comedy of manners "The Second Man" was successfully produced on Broadway, and his financial worries were over. His long dramatic and literary career included, in addition to his many comedies, screen plays for "Queen Christina" and "Anna Karenina," biographies of Lord Duveen and Max Beerbohm, a novel and two memoirs.

Genuine wit is rare on our stage; we have lived in the age of the wisecrack. The latter is apt to be a put-down, like Groucho Marx's "I never forget a face, but I'm going to make an exception with yours." Wit is more in the nature of an interchange, as this between Lord Illingworth and Mrs. Allonby in "A Woman of no Importance":

LORD ILLINGWORTH:
Shall we go into tea?

MRS. ALLONBY:
Do you like simple pleasures?

LORD ILLINGWORTH:
I adore simple pleasures. They are the last refuge of the complex. But, if you wish, let us stay here. The Book of Life begins with a man and woman in a garden.

MRS. ALLONBY:
It ends with Revelations.

Behrman is our wittiest playwright since Oscar Wilde. But where Wilde, writing in a British era of sumptuous self-assurance, could indulge in the freest comic whimsy, this was not practicable for Behrman, whose comedies appeared on Broadway in the nineteen-thirties, in a time of deep depression and the rumblings of social change and the threats of revolution and dictators. As John Anderson wrote in his introduction to the published edition of "Wine of Choice":

> . . . he knows there is more to society than the social pages in the paper; his plays retain the glossiness of veneer without being shallow . . . For Mr. Behrman's greater fate was to be born into a time when the essential material for comedy transcends the mere social aspects of manners that glitter in the English classics . . . For the brilliance of these comedies lies in the clarity of the characters and their understanding of the world they live in. It is a world, for the most part, of strict manners and loose morals, a world superbly cut for a master of comedy, since it shuns the heart and lives serenely in the head.

"Wine of Choice," produced in 1938, is the Behrman comedy *par excellence*. In it, dialogue is all. In some of his plays he has created a straw man to riddle with his wit: the absurdly self-absorbed and dictatorial father in "The Talley Method"; the misguided author of brilliant parlor comedies who wants to waste his talent on a "soulful" tragedy in "No Time for Comedy"; the shallow egotist in "The Second Man." If the "message" in these dramas is something less than weighty, the sparkling lines make up for it. So why do we even need a basic human problem to hang the wit on?

We don't. In "Wine of Choice" we listen, and that is enough, to the thought and laughter-provoking chatter of the guests in the Long Island cottage of Binkie Niebuhr (played appropriately in the original production by Alexander Wooll-cott): the stout, self-indulgent, all-contriving, all-observing, cynical and innovative middle-aged bachelor whose sole joy and activity is manipulating, for their at least worldly benefit, the lives and careers of his rich or talented friends. If he is something less of an idealist than Behrman himself, many of his aphorisms might be those of his creator. The hero, Ryder, modeled on Bronson Cutting, the rich but altruistic New Yorker who became a liberal senator from New Mexico, is surely the character whom Behrman most admires, but we suspect there is some of the author in Binkie's retort:

> ... there are saints who will go to the stake rather than pronounce a meaningless word in two syllables rather than one. There are even people like Ryder who are under the illusion that bribing Spaniards in New Mexico is more exalted than bribing saloon keepers in New York.

Binkie's philosophy is expressed in his statement: "I try to re-create the world. I try to make a world in which instinct is subordinate to reason."

Behrman, however, was always acutely aware of the threat to reason, a seemingly fatal one on the eve of World War II, of the twin menaces of Stalin and Hitler. Chris, the young communist in the play, is depicted as a fanatical red, entirely willing, even eager, to liquidate his opponents. Other than a brief attraction to the heroine he exhibits no humanity, and in the end he and Ryder sharpen the issue between them.

CHRIS:
There is a code among parasites as there is a code among thieves.

RYDER:
I would defend it with my blood!

CHRIS:
You will have to defend it with your blood.

Behrman has great sympathy for the weaknesses of his always intelligent characters. His artists and writers know that they never scale the peaks (does that reflect a modest estimate of his own talents?), but they reconcile themselves to their less exalted status. It would surely be foolish not to. As Storey says in "The Second Man": "Most suffering is the bunk. Unintelligent people who want things beyond their limitations." And the painter Marian Froude in "Biography" defends her flattering portraits of the great against the charge of parasitism thus: "Isn't there in biology something about benevolent parasites? Many great men, I believe, owe a debt to their parasites, as many plants do . . . there are varieties." Her realistic acceptance of the world is described in a stagenote: ". . . the tears in things have warmed without scalding her; she floats through life like a dancer's scarf in perpetual enjoyment of its colors and contours."

The problem of Storey in "The Second Man" is the problem of the civilized, perhaps the overcivilized world as Behrman sees it:

MONICA:
Old! You're not.

STOREY:

I am. There's someone else inside me — a second man, a cynical, odious person, who keeps watching me, who keeps listening to what I say, grinning and sophisticated, horrid . . . He never lets me be — this other man . . .

MONICA:

Kill him.

STOREY:

I can't kill him. He'll outlive me.

Behrman wrote his finest play when he at last created a character who lived aside from the wit: Leonie Frothingham in "End of Summer," of whom Marian Froude in "Biography" may have been a preliminary sketch. Here is how Behrman describes her and how all her lines show her and how the incomparable Ina Claire played her in 1936:

There is something, for all her gaiety, heartbreaking about Leonie, something childish and child-like — an acceptance of people instantly and uncritically at the best of their own valuation. She is impulsive and warm-hearted and generous to a fault. Her own fragile and exquisite loveliness she offers to the world half-shyly, tentatively, bearing it like a cup containing a precious liquid of which not a drop must be spilled. A spirituelle amoureuse, she is repelled by the gross or the voluptuary; this is not hypocrisy — it is, in Leonie, a more serious defect than that. In the world in which she moves hypocrisy is merely a social lubricant, but this myopia — alas for Leonie! — springs from a congenital and temperamental inability to face any but the pleasantest and most immediately appealing and the most flattering aspects of things — in life and in her own nature. At this moment, though, she is the loveliest fabrication of Nature, happy in the summer sun and loving all the world.

And when Paula Frothingham, to save her mother from falling the victim of the oily, fortune-hunting psychiatrist with whom Leonie is in love, exposes the doctor's double game with mother and daughter, there is near tragedy in Leonie's piteous retort: "This isn't very nice of you, Paula."

Behrman has been compared with Congreve, and the comparison is apt. It is both interesting and exhilarating to read "The Way of the World" after "Wine of Choice" or "Rain from Heaven." It is at once abundantly clear that Congreve's stage world is entirely self-enclosed. If any of his audience was worried about the territorial ambitions of Louis XIV (the date is 1700), there is no sign of it in the dialogue. And I'm afraid the comedy benefits from this. We can relax in a London of lust and swagger and ebullient cynicism where Mirabell and Millamant represent all that is most admired in both sexes. Does it bother us that Mirabell has arranged a marriage between the widow whom he believes he has impregnated but whom he does not wish to wed, and an unsuspecting bachelor acquaintance of his? No, because the hoodwinked bridegroom is a bit of a cad and in no way the equal of such a handsome, witty and gallant Restoration buck as Mirabell. And what about his concern with Millamant's fortune? Well, if that wasn't the way of the world, what was? We are as one with the rest of the cast, who are simply fortunate to be able to match their wits against those of the two charming lovers.

Will we ever again see a world where a cultivated audience can enjoy a comedy quite so socially irresponsible? Perhaps not. And perhaps we shouldn't want to. Think of all the people who *should* have been on the consciences of English playgoers in 1700!

Robert E. Sherwood

꒛ ꒛ ꒛

I N MANY WAYS Robert Emmet Sherwood (1896–1955) had
the happiest of lives. Born into a rich, congenial and distinguished family, he was an attractive and popular man, with a
brilliant wit and the talent to carve effective drama out of even
the most unpromising material. His plays were almost invariably Broadway hits; "Idiot's Delight" and "Abe Lincoln in Illinois" won him Pulitzer Prizes. He pleased both the multitude
and the critics, and he made a great deal of money. He even
managed to write (sometimes with co-authors) the screenplays
for twenty-two movies, including "The Scarlet Pimpernel,"
"Marie-Antoinette" and "The Ghost Goes West."

But the culminating experience of this favored lifetime
came in World War II, when he was a principal speech writer
and frequent companion of President Roosevelt, whom he
admired above all men, with a ringside seat to the great
drama of the globe, which excited him almost as much as his
own plays. And when it was all over, in triumph and tragedy,
he was able to make his most lasting contribution to history
and literature in the memoir *Roosevelt and Hopkins*, which
gained him a third Pulitzer.

That was one side of his story. Of course, there was
another. Sherwood's parents may not have seen the wicked

witch at his christening, but they should have known she was lurking somewhere. All his life he was to suffer from self-doubt and depression. His health was never good, and he had recurrent attacks of an agonizing *tic douloureux*. His first marriage, to a selfish spendthrift, was a miserable one, and his second, though happy, was at bitter expense to his conscience: he took his best friend's wife. In the First World War he had to endure five months of hell in the trenches, serving in the Canadian Black Watch battalion (he had been turned down by the U.S. Army), which left him with a load of terrible memories. As his able biographer, John Mason Brown, put it: "He could not get the war's broken promises and betrayed ideals out of his mind. The war made him a pacifist; the peace, a pessimist. His deepening conviction was that a dark present was leading to a darker future."

Brown, moving on to the effect of his subject's experiences in the Second World War, describes how gaunt and gloomy Sherwood appeared in 1954, shortly before his death, at age fifty-nine, making a speech at his alma mater, Milton Academy, in Boston:

It was the accumulated weariness of days and nights and years of living and giving and working as if his superb energies were endless. It was the secret fear that haunts the creator, the fear which tormented Sherwood, the fear that his gift had left him because he had not had a successful new play produced on Broadway in fourteen years.

It was the sorrow and the emptiness of the letdown after the death of Roosevelt and after the dizzying tensions and excitements of the war years spent close to the White House and to great events. It was the heartbreak of seeing the heroic efforts and sacrifices of a Second Great World War end in disenchantment, with Hitler and other marchers stopped, but with victory not even bringing a true peace. It was the deep alarm with which he recognized the threats of nuclear power and his realization that this time he spoke not only in a different world but in a different age.

I am never sure how deeply any individual is affected by world tragedy. Doctor Johnson opined that public affairs vex no man, and there were nine years between the day of the Milton speech and the end of World War II. I suspect that the darkness of Sherwood's state of mind came more from the drop in his dramatic creativity than from any world crisis. And what was the cause of this drop? I think Brown gives us a clue in the subtitle of his illuminating biography. To *The Worlds of Robert Sherwood* he added the words "Mirror to His Times." It may be that Sherwood had suspected that such a mirror was just what he had ceased to be.

There was never much question from the beginning that Sherwood's life was going to be centered on the theatre, whether as a writer, producer, director, critic or actor, or all five. The last-named was eliminated by the height he ultimately attained: six feet, seven inches. He used to explain the U.S. Army's rejection of him on the military's fear of having to dig a trench in France deep enough for him. As a boy and as a college student he was always producing plays and acting in them, and his leaving Harvard to enlist in the Black Watch probably anticipated what would have been his expulsion for low grades. He was passionately pro-Ally and anti-German; disillusionment was to come with the betrayal of the peace at Versailles. As Brown put it: "From boyhood he was not only an idealist and a romantic but on occasion an unblushing sentimentalist who believed in heroes, needed them and was lucky enough to find them."

For all his love of drama, however, he was late in becoming a professional playwright. "The Road to Rome" was not produced until 1927, after eight years largely devoted to the writing of movie criticism. The play was a historical comedy with serious overtones; it portrayed how the lovely Greek wife of the Roman dictator saved his besieged city from the sack of the Carthaginian army by spending a night of love in Hannibal's tent and convincing him that war is futile. The play, like all of Sherwood's, is full of wit — he was not for nothing a charter member of the Algonquin Round Table — but the philosophizing of Amytis, the heroine, and of her converted conqueror is banal, to say the least. When Hannibal protests: "I came to conquer Rome; anything short of that is failure," she responds: "Are you sure of that? Are you sure that you didn't come all this way to find your own soul?"

Sherwood in all of his hits would continue this note of half-baked romantic idealism, when it wasn't half-baked romantic despair. "Abe Lincoln in Illinois" is saved from it by the fact that many if not most of the Great Emancipator's lines are taken from his own writings. John Mason Brown in his review of the play noted that the sixteenth president should have taken a curtain call with Sherwood. But in "The Petrified Forest" the hero, Alan Squier, tells the heroine: "You see — the trouble with me is, I belong to a vanishing race. I'm one of the intellectuals . . . Brains without purpose. Noise without sound. Shadow without substance." He goes on to explain that the intellectuals were wrong when they thought they had conquered Nature and dammed her up and sold her in cellophane. Now Nature was hitting back.

Not with the old weapons — floods, plagues, holocausts. We can neutralize them. She's fighting back with strange instruments called neuroses. She's deliberately afflicting mankind with the jitters. Nature is proving that she can't be beaten, not by the likes of us. She's taking the world away from the intellectuals and giving it back to the apes.

"Idiot's Delight," with its villainous munitions maker and its clash of tin-pan patriots, tells us nothing about the origins of modern warfare that every member of the audience does not already know and deplore. God is described by the heroine, Irene: "Poor lonely old soul. Sitting up in heaven with nothing to do but play solitaire. Poor dear God. Playing Idiot's Delight. The game that never means anything and never ends." And "There Shall Be No Night" is a sweet threnody, on the fate of unhappy Finland invaded by powerful Russia, which was cynically and successfully converted into a hit about an anonymous victim nation when the Soviets became our allies.

Why then were these plays so successful? Because Sherwood was a master in the art of the theatre; his plays are not only tense and exciting; they are uproariously funny. And because also, it must be added, of Alfred Lunt and Lynn Fontanne. Never forget that glorious acting pair, forever associated with "Reunion in Vienna," "Idiot's Delight" and "There Shall Be No Night." As Brown says:

> The Lunts as he [Sherwood] well knew, were perfectionists, always eager to better what they were doing. For Sherwood this was one of the joys and challenges of working with them. He welcomed, or nearly always welcomed, the comments or suggestions of the Lunts, recognizing that these were not so much criticisms as creative acts of collaboration.

Sherwood himself candidly recognized the superiority in his plays of treatment over theme: "The trouble with me is that I start with a big message and end up with nothing but good entertainment." And Brown, never one to underestimate the magic of make believe, added:

He wanted the theater to be the theater. He did not want it to reject its special possibilities as a medium. He wanted it to rejoice in them, unashamed of sentiment, unafraid of glamor, unintimidated by romance, a release for the emotions, a dispenser of wonder.

All of which helps to explain why Sherwood was for his day only and not for all time. He was, however, to be even more closely for his own day during the Second World War. "There Shall Be No Night" expressed his renunciation of pacifism before the threat of the new barbarians. His was the reaction of untold thousands of intellectuals who had vowed that the Armistice of 1918 should be the true end of carnage. The unmitigated evil of the dictatorships had roused them once more to arms. The free world was united in what seemed a kind of crusade. The feeling is hard for generations disillusioned by corrupt politics and cruel and bungled wars to comprehend.

Sherwood commemorated the era in *Roosevelt and Hopkins*, his most distinguished and lasting work. The nostalgia that we feel for those days may be tinged with envy. It would be nice, perhaps, to believe that strongly in something again. Perhaps a sense of the time is best conveyed in Sherwood's description of FDR going to work on a wartime morning in the White House:

After the session in the President's bedroom, Rosenman and I went over to the Cabinet Room to await the summons. The signal bells announced the President's approach to his office and we stood by the French windows leading out to the colonnade and watched him go by in his armless, cushionless, uncomfortable wheelchair, pushed by his Negro valet, Chief Petty Officer Arthur Prettyman. Accompanying him was the detail of Secret Service men, some of them carrying the large, overflowing wire baskets of papers on which he had been working the night before and the dispatches that had come in the morning. When Fala came abreast of the wheelchair as it rolled along, Roosevelt would reach down and scratch his neck. This progress to the day's work by a crippled man was a sight to stir the most torpid imagination; for here was a clear glimpse of the Roosevelt that the people believed him to be — the chin up, the cigarette holder tilted at what was always described as "a jaunty angle" and the air of irrepressible confidence that whatever problems the day might bring, he would find a way to handle them. The fact that this confidence was not always justified made it none the less authentic and reassuring. When I saw the President go by on these mornings, I felt that nobody who worked for him had a right to feel tired.

IRIS ORIGO

꙯ ꙯ ꙯

HENRY JAMES wrote of the Brontë sisters:

The romantic tradition of the Brontës, with posterity, has
been still more essentially helped, I think, by a force independent of any one of their applied faculties — by the
attendant image of their dreary, their tragic history, their
loneliness and poverty of life.

The personal position of the three sisters, in short, has
become the very tone of their united production.

In somewhat the same fashion the privileged position of
Iris Origo (1902–1988) has become a part of her literary
work. It is as rare as it is wonderful to see a person, born and
bred with every advantage — educational, personal, financial
and social — use each advantage to its fullest capacity. Origo
was like the man in the parable who turned his five talents
into ten.

She was the only child of Bayard Cutting, a sensitive and
intellectual American millionaire, who died young of tubercu-
losis (her one disadvantage) and left her a fortune. The Cuttings were old New York, but unlike the denizens of Edith

Wharton's "age of innocence," they were a family of great cultivation and artistic tastes. Origo's grandmother Olivia Murray Cutting, in her extreme old age, told the writer of this piece, then young, of a summer in the White Mountains in 1865 when she had wanted to go for a hike with three young men who were visiting her family. Her father protested that they didn't want the company of a little girl, but one of them insisted, "Oh, let her come, please," and she went. The three young men were William and Henry James and the future Justice Oliver Wendell Holmes, Jr.

Origo's mother was English, Lady Sybil Cuffe, the daughter of an Irish peer, the Earl of Desart, a witty and talented woman, but self-centered and demanding and something of a *malade imaginaire*. The young Cuttings lived much in Europe in a vain search for places favorable to Bayard's health, and little Iris was later to pay a price for her multilingual education. If her mother on a train journey smelled cigar smoke, Iris would be sent to seek out the culprit.

She described one such incident in her memoirs, *Images and Shadows* (1970):

"Darling, I am sure I smelled a cigar. *Would* you mind explaining to the man — no, not in the next carriage, I think it must be three or four doors off — that I am very delicate . . ."

I did mind. I minded so much that I would stand outside the offender's compartment praying for an accident before I had to go in.

"I am so sorry but my mother . . ." "*Scusi tanto, ma mia Madre* . . ." "*Verzeihen Sie* . . ." "*Veuillez m'excuser* . . ."

Sometimes my interlocutor was nice about it, and sometimes not. If he went on smoking, I would hurry back to our compartment, shut the door, hand my mother a book, and retreat in silent prayer that she would not notice, but in vain. A few moments later:

"Darling, I don't think you *can* have explained yourself properly. Would you call the conductor?"

I wished that I were dead.

Origo escaped the maternal demands, at least partially, when she made an early marriage to an Italian marchese, Antonio Origo, and together they managed a vast tract of farms near Florence, with winters in Rome. Iris was not only a successful wife and mother and an efficient estate manager; she became a Greek and Latin scholar, a historical researcher, a heroine in the war and the author of a series of beautiful books.

It did not look, however, as if such a future awaited her when she was a lonely fatherless child isolated in the splendor of the Villa Medici in Fiesole, which her mother had bought and in which she gave constant parties that could hardly include a small daughter. But a good friend intervened to save her.

At the age of twelve . . . a piece of great good fortune befell me. Bernard Berenson, to whom I shall always be grateful, advised my mother to let me receive a classical education and even supplied me with the name of the brilliant tutor with whom I worked for the next three years. Professor Solone Monti. It was with him that I spent the happiest hours of my girlhood — perhaps the happiest I have ever known.

And then Virgil came into her life.

For the first time I became aware of poetry as something not disconnected with life, but incorporated in it, and also realized how profoundly the classical tradition was still rooted in the Mediterranean world — transmitted not only in the cadences of words, but in nature itself and in the most familiar objects of daily use. As I looked around me, there was nothing in sight that Virgil himself might not have seen: the olive trees and figs and vines, the fat-bellied gourd trailing in the grass, the single clump of lilies beside the farm door, the pungent thyme beneath our feet, the oxen plodding slowly home, the goat . . . even the wooden flails leaning against one of the walls of the amphitheatre, the small curved sickle with which a bare-armed, dark-skinned girl was cutting a bundle of grass and the round bee-hives placed, as the poet advised, beside a little channel of running water.

Iris was safe now. She would always have the world of letters.

War in Val d'Orcia (1947), which is probably Origo's most widely read book, differs from her other work in that it involves neither scholarship nor art but is simply the exact transcript of the journal that she kept in the years 1941 to 1944, when the Origos' farms near Florence were the scene of continuous warfare. The Germans had given up the south of Italy, but they were determined to hold the north against the invading Allied armies; the Origos had to deal with their officers in order to keep the latters' appropriation of vital supplies to a minimum so that the land could support and feed the dozens of tenants who lived on it and the refugee families from bombed-out areas who poured into every barn or structure available. Their task was not made easier by their decision to give aid, at constant risk of their and their two baby daughters' lives, to the many men hiding in the woods and hills: escaped Allied prisoners of war, Italian youths avoiding the draft of their disintegrating pro-German government, and anti-Fascist partisans who recklessly sniped at Germans without regard to the hideous reprisals taken on the civilian population.

In part to preserve her own balance and sanity, Origo kept a journal of her weekly activities, hiding it away at night among the children's books in the nursery. It is a thrilling story. We read of German officers who were cultivated and almost charming, of Germans who were fanatically Nazi to the end, and of Germans who were simply brutes. We read of Fascists who were viler than the vilest Germans, of spies and sadists. We read of peasants who risked their lives daily to hide British soldiers, of whose nation and war effort they knew almost nothing. And what is nearly as fascinating is the twisted picture of the war on other fronts as it filtered into this isolated area: the rumors of devastating new German weapons, the desolate tales of refugees, the constant whispers of terrible defeats or incredible victories, the snatched bits of radio news, the threats and boasts of the jittery occupying forces.

And at last, unbelievably, it was over. The first British troops arrived. The friendly, assured, familiar sound of an English voice — the tone of Albion, sanity in the midst of madness — accosted the ears of the secret journalist. "Are you the Marchese Origo? The whole Eighth Army has been looking for you."

Returning to her home, which had been temporarily vacated as a battle site, Origo found a lost friend.

I go back into the farm, and there, crouching under a sofa, I see a black shadow. I whistle, and, half incredulously, he crawls out, then leaps upon me in wild delight, and from that minute never leaves my side. It is Gambolino, the poodle, miraculously safe, but pitifully thin, and so nervy that the slightest noise sends him trembling under the nearest bed.

Origo's talents found their widest scope in *Leopardi* (1953), where the skillfully edited letters of her subject and her own powerful evocations of small-town Italian life in the first decades of the nineteenth century form a seamless unit. The cloistered, scholastic early existence of the melancholy poet, an undersized and sickly hunchback, in the dreary palazzo of his noble but hard-up parents provides a long and richly detailed prelude to the story of his partial escape into romantic poetry and his ultimate relapse into depression and an early death. Origo makes him constantly interesting; she cannot make him appealing.

Unknown to him were sheer animal exuberance and heedlessness, those gifts of physical well-being which sheathe our nerves with a deceptive sense of false security.

Leopardi himself set this seal on his life:

I gave myself up entirely to the terrifying and barbarous joy of despair.

Immersed in self-pity, he was not able even, after his escape from his home town, Recanati, in the Papal States on the Adriatic, to join his new friends in Bologna and Florence in their schemes to free Italy from its scourge of petty tyrants. He confined his patriotism to his passionate poetry, which received an early acclaim. Mankind, he maintained, occupied too small a space in the universe for him to be overly concerned about it.

Nor was he attractive, either in his person or his habits. His friends had to put up "with his headaches, his constipation, his insomnia and with his increasing complaints about the cold, the heat, the light and the noise." He also had an irritating habit of cracking his finger bones (the *crepitous digitorum* of the Romans); his clothes were spotted with food stains, and he insisted on airless dark rooms, for his eyes.

Origo, however, brings out the charm that he could exercise in conversation, and cites his friends' unanimous approval of his "sweet, heavenly smile." And when we learn that his fanatical bigot of a mother was thankful when she lost a baby, who would thus escape such adult temptations as might place paradise for the infant at risk, and that, when Leopardi appeared in the streets of Recanati, he was apt to be greeted by snowballs or stones flung by urchins screaming "Hunchback!" we can feel almost as sorry for him as he did for himself.

Indeed, his feelings seem to have been little spared. Niccolò Tommaseo, the Florentine Catholic scholar, summed up the poet's philosophy as: "There's no god because I'm a hunchback; I'm a hunchback because there's no god." Actually, Leopardi seemed at times to question his own agnosticism. As Origo observes: "It's not easy for a man to destroy entirely what has once stirred his spirit, and most men have some secret altar in their hearts, dedicated to the fallen gods."

Towards its close the biography has a fine example of how Origo can juxtapose a vivid cityscape with a tart example of Latin crudity to evoke a picture of Italy itself:

Florence in midsummer becomes a deserted city. Its inhabitants, if they have not been able to escape to the seaside or the neighboring hills, take refuge from the heat behind closed shutters. During the long hours of the afternoon no one dares venture into the glare of the Lungarno, between the dazzling river and the torrid heat of the sun-baked palazzi. Even in the dark cool avenues of the Cascine no sound breaks the stillness but the strident crackling of the cicadas; the air is heavy with the scent of limes and hazy with white dust. Then, in the tension of that summer heat, every nerve is quivering; every sense becomes more alive than usual, every feeling more intense — and in his room alone the poet dreamed of Aspasia.

But this Aspasia, his last, Fanny Targioni, came no nearer to succumbing to the sick man's appeals than had any of the others. When, decades later, the novelist Matilde Serao asked Fanny how she could have resisted so great a romantic poet, the old lady replied, "My dear, he stank."

Origo's most valuable contribution to literary scholarship is *Byron, the Last Attachment* (1949), whose subtitle is "The Story of Byron and Teresa Guiccioli as Told by Their Unpublished Letters and Other Family Papers." The documents, long held by the Guiccioli family under lock and key, were made available to Origo by Count Carlo Gama, Teresa's great nephew, and although her editorship is masterly, the bulk of the book is the writing of the two lovers and not a true part of the Origo canon.

Much more of her writing is to be found in *The Merchant of Prato* (1957), which Origo put together out of the remarkably complete archives of one Francesco Datini, a fifteenth-century Italian merchant. There is nothing of any particular interest about Datini himself. He was a tough-minded businessman, of greater than average imagination, who was willing to take substantial risks in shipping goods abroad over pirate- and storm-infested waters and in establishing branches in towns other than his native Prato. He cheated on his always complaining wife and, with surprising patience, put up with the lifelong sermonizing of a priggish letter-writing friend who found him too grossly materialistic. The only really exciting thing about Datini is how much we know about him. His archives contain every detail of his business and private life. He is like one of those preserved figures in the ruins of Pompeii, caught in their death throes. We marvel that he is there.

Origo does not attempt to make him more than he was. She uses him as the window through which to view the whole life of a fifteenth-century community. We see every detail of his house, his household, his slaves, his business transactions, his friends, his religious practices. We have the experience of living in a totally different age.

Origo also wrote a charming short study of Allegra, the bastard daughter of Byron and Claire Clairmont, who died at the age of five. The poor child was the subject of bitter fights between the parents, who rarely saw her, and expired at last abandoned in a convent. Origo endows her final scene with some of the pathos of the one that Lytton Strachey provided for Queen Victoria:

> Yes, it had been bewildering, the world as she had known it, a world that had contained the formidable capacious person that was Papa, the Mama who came and went, who kissed and clutched her too hard, the prim, sour Mrs. Hoppner, the loud-voiced Fornarina and pretty Teresa, the masked figures at the Ravenna carnival, and finally the strict, quiet, gentle Capuchin nuns. Now only they were left.

There remains to be mentioned Origo's life of San Bernardino (1962), the fifteenth-century Sienese preacher who assembled mammoth crowds wherever he went and who was revered by emperor and pope as well as by the poor and wretched. What was the nature of his gift?

> The outstanding gift which drew so many thousands to hear him, and often changed their lives, was surely one 0to which Dante had already given a name — *l'intelletto d'amore* (the understanding of love). He understood men and women to whom he spoke, and he understood them because he loved them.

As the saint put it himself: "You must suffer in your own self the pain of the man who is being hanged. You must feel yourself what Christ felt on the cross."

But here even Iris Origo cannot persuade me to bridge the gap between the eras. I wonder whether San Bernardino felt the flames that licked the flesh of the witches and homosexuals whom he helped to send to the stake.